Social Justice and the Constitution

Perspectives on a Social Union for Canada

The Carleton Library Series

A series of original works, new collections and reprints of source material relating to Canada, issued under the supervision of the Editorial Board, Carleton Library Series, Carleton University Press Inc., Ottawa, Canada.

AUGUSTANA LIBRARY
UNIVERSITY OF ALBERTA

Centre for Constitutional Studies

Social Justice
and the
Constitution

Perspectives on a Social Union for Canada

Edited by

Joel Bakan

&

David Schneiderman

Carleton University Press

Ottawa, Canada

1992

Centre d'études

constitutionnelles

CARLETON UNIVERSITY 1942-1992

ISBN   0-88629-195-X (paperback)
ISBN   0-88629-196-8 (casebound)

Printed and bound in Canada

Carleton Library Series #175

Canadian Cataloguing in Publication Data

Main entry under title:
        Social Justice and the Constitution: perspectives on a social union for Canada

(Carleton library series; 175)
Includes bibliographical references.
ISBN 0-88629-196-8 (bound) – ISBN 0-88629-195-X (pbk.)

        1. Social legislation–Canada. 2. Canada–Social policy.
3. Canada–Constitutional law–Amendments.
I. Schneiderman, David, 1958- . II. Bakan, Joel, 1959-.
III. Series.

HN103.5.S624 1992   344.71   C92-090688-5

Distributed by   Oxford University Press Canada
                 70 Wynford Drive
                 Don Mills, Ontario
                 Canada. M3C 1J9
                 (416) 441-2941

Cover design: Melanie Eastley

Acknowledgements

Carleton University Press gratefully acknowledges the support extended to its publishing programme by the Canada Council and the Ontario Arts Council.

Contents

Contributors

Joel Bakan teaches at the Faculty of Law, University of British Columbia. He writes and has published widely in the areas of constitutional law and theory with a focus on questions about the politics and ideology of rights.

Gwen Brodsky is retained as counsel at the British Columbia Public Interest Advocacy Centre, where she has a practice in equality rights law. Ms. Brodsky represents women and members of other marginalized groups in test case litigation. Ms. Brodsky's publications include *Canadian Charter Equality Rights for Women: One Step Forward or Two Steps Back?* (Canadian Advisory Council on the Status of Women), a comprehensive analysis of the early years of equality rights litigation, co-authored with Shelagh Day.

Glenn Drover teaches social policy at the School of Social Work, University of British Columbia. He has written widely in the social welfare field. His two most recent books are *Welfare and Worker Participation* with Patrick Kerans (Macmillan) and *Free Trade and Social Policy* (Canadian Council on Social Development). Currently he is working on a book about theories on social well-being.

Harry J. Glasbeek, Professor of Law, Osgoode Hall Law School, York University, writes mainly in the areas of labour relations law, corporate criminality and occupational health and safety. Since 1981, he has developed an unhealthy interest in constitutional rights and has written a number of articles on the subject.

Martha Jackman is an Associate Professor in the French Language Common Law Program at the University of Ottawa, where she teaches constitutional law and feminist legal theory. In addition to her research and writing on the *Charter* and welfare rights, she was involved in drafting the National Anti-Poverty Organization's alternative social charter.

Lucie Lamarche est avocat et associée à l'étude Saint-Louis, Lippel, Guillet et Lamarche de Montréal. Elle est par ailleurs professeure de droit social au Département des Sciences juridiques de l'Université du Québec à Montréal. Elle complète actuellement une thèse de doctorat qu'elle déposera auprès de la Faculté de droit de l'Université libre de Bruxelles portant sur le thème du droit au travail et du droit international des droits sociaux et économiques de la personne.

Hester Lessard is an assistant professor at the University of Victoria Faculty of Law. Her areas of research are constitutional law and feminist legal theories.

Jennifer Nedelsky teaches at the Faculty of Law and Department of Political Science at the University of Toronto. She is the author of *Private Property and the Limits of American Constitutionalism: The Madisonian Framework and its Legacy* (Chicago: University of Chicago Press, 1990).

David Schneiderman is Executive Director of the Centre for Constitutional Studies at the University of Alberta. He has published and teaches in the area of constitutional law and has also edited *Freedom of Expression and the Charter* (Carswell) and *Conversations: Women and Constitutional Reform* (Center for Constitutional Studies).

Craig Scott has been Assistant Professor of Law at the University of Toronto since 1989. His research centres on international legal theory, notably in the area of human rights, as well as comparative constitutional law; within these fields, he has concentrated on questions related to the conceptualization and protection of social rights. He is currently working on a book tentatively titled *Bearing Rights and Being Human: Human Rights Discourse in International Law.*

Acknowledgements

The idea for this book arose initially at a conference of the Critical Legal Network at Harvard University and Northeastern University Law Schools in May 1992. A few of the authors first presented their papers at that conference. The book quickly took shape thanks to the cooperation of the authors, all of whom agreed to produce their texts on short notice and to keep them current in a period of rapid constitutional change.

We are grateful to the Centre for Constitutional Studies at the University of Alberta who agreed to coordinate the project. The Centre is able to carry on such activities thanks to the generous financial support of the Alberta Law Foundation. Christine Urquhart, Executive Assistant at the Centre for Constitutional Studies, helped to carry the project to completion with the able assistance of Ardis Kolot, Debra MacGregor, Craig McDougall and Lu Ziola. Michael Gnarowski at Carleton University Press deserves special thanks for his continued and unflagging support of the project. Steven Uriarte at the Press is also to be thanked for helping to get the book to press so quickly and efficiently. Patrick Macklem provided helpful comments about the manuscript.

We would be remiss if we did not thank our respective institutional homes for their support: the Faculty of Law at the University of British Columbia and the Faculty of Law at the University of Alberta (home to the Centre for Constitutional Studies).

J.B.

D.S.

October 1992

1

Introduction

Joel Bakan and David Schneiderman

In the fall of 1990, the New Democratic Party, the official political voice of the left in Canada, was elected in Ontario. Soon after, in the spring of 1991, the idea of entrenching a charter of social rights in the Constitution was raised in the Ontario legislature; this was followed by release of a series of discussion papers on the idea in the fall of 1991. Also, in the fall of 1991 there were electoral victories for the NDP in Saskatchewan and British Columbia, and this ensured the party a powerful presence in ongoing constitutional negotiations. The idea of a constitutional charter of social rights now had some prospect of becoming a reality. Most recently, Canadians were asked to endorse a set of proposals for constitutional amendment, the Charlottetown Accord, which includes a "social union" provision modelled on Ontario's original proposal. The Accord was rejected in a national referendum. Despite this, we believe the idea of a social charter is likely to remain part of Canadian constitutional politics and the politics of the legal protection of human rights, more generally.

This volume is about the debate among progressive scholars and activists that began with the Ontario proposal and continued with the Charlottetown Accord's social union provision. The volume has two broad purposes: first, to analyze the social union proposal and to look at issues concerning its monitoring and enforcement. The second and perhaps more important purpose is to analyze the range of political and theoretical arguments developed among progressive people in response to the prospect of entrenching social welfare protections in the Constitution. The social charter debate has raised the difficult question of the relationship between law and social change, one much considered with the civil and political rights of the *Charter of Rights and Freedoms*. But it has done so in the novel context (novel, at least for North America) of *social* rights. The authors of this collection are all committed to the advancement of social justice, but they have different views on the role of a social charter or union in pursuing that end.

The social charter idea did not come out of nowhere. It emerged at a historical moment of interaction between two political occurrences in Canada – the demise of the social welfare state, and severe constitutional instability. Understanding why and how the social charter idea developed requires a brief (albeit incomplete) historical sketch. The idea of a constitutional social charter or union is a new one in Canada, but the practice of using law to create and enforce social benefits, and impose social obligations on governments and private actors, is not new. The social charter idea developed against the backdrop of a progressive legalization of social welfare throughout most of the twentieth century. Social legislation can be traced back at least to the Poor Law of 1601,[1] but its systematic use is largely a product of this century. In Canada, from the 1840s until 1914 there developed a variety of church-based and other voluntary charitable institutions. It was only after WW1, however, that the Canadian state began to play a significant role in promoting social welfare.[2] By the 1920s, social welfare programs were the subject of much legislative activity, and an Old Age Pension program, the first "significant" national shared-cost initiative, was introduced in 1927.[3]

The ravages of the "Great Depression" led to greater involvement of the Canadian state in spending and regulating to advance social welfare. Local governments largely were incapable of controlling or thwarting the effects of the market crash,[4] and national governments were called upon to enact measures to protect the interests of unemployed people and working people. A "new deal" legislative package was put together by R.B. Bennett's government in 1935 providing for social security, unemployment relief, and minimum wages and maximum hours, among other forms of protection. Not unpredictably, the Judicial Committee of the Privy Council struck down the legislation, holding in a series of decisions that the package was *ultra vires* the Parliament of Canada under the constitutional division of powers.[5] The effect of these decisions was partly mitigated in 1940 when the *British North America Act* was amended to give the federal government jurisdiction over unemployment relief. The *Unemployment Insurance Act* was introduced shortly thereafter.

The years between the wars saw other programs, such as mother's allowance and grants for housing construction, introduced by the federal government.[6] Following WWII, the Canadian social welfare state went through a period of rapid and substantial change due to the need for economic and social reconstruction, and the rise of radicalized trade unions, the Co-operative Commonwealth Federation (CCF), and later the NDP.[7] The 1942 Report of Lord Beveridge, the architect of the British welfare state, was a bestseller in Canada. Leonard Marsh was commissioned to produce a report of similar scope for Canada, a major recommendation of which – family allowances – was followed by the Mackenzie King government.[8] Not too long after, calls emerged in Parliament to establish a national health care scheme. However, it was only after a medicare program was developed and tested in 1961 by the CCF Premier of Saskatchewan, Tommy Douglas, that other provinces co-operated with the federal government to establish a national program. This effort culminated in the enactment of the federal *National Health Care Act*, which formalized a scheme of conditional grants to the provinces to support the financing of health care.

The Liberal governments of Lester Pearson and Pierre Elliott Trudeau, through the sixties and early seventies, were responsible for putting in place the modern social welfare state in Canada. The programs established or modified during this time "included the Canada Pension Plan (1965), the National Medical Care Insurance Act (1966), the Canada Assistance Plan (1966), the Department of Regional Economic Expansion (1969), the Unemployment Insurance Act (1971), Tax Reforms (1973), and a Family Allowance Act (1973)."[9] These were all initiated at the federal level, though some of them involved shared-cost arrangements with the provinces. At the same time, throughout the twentieth century the provinces had introduced a wide variety of social policy measures, including workers' compensation and health and safety laws, education programs, employment standards, and human rights protection, without assistance from the federal government. These regulatory programs were substantially developed in the postwar period.

Many of the social programs and regulations developed over the last century, whether they were federal, provincial or shared between the two levels of government, now have attained a measure of sacrosanctity. They are considered part of the panoply of rights and privileges attaching to Canadian citizenship. There has been a movement from private charity to public rights, and the corresponding growth of a public expectation that the state meet basic needs of its citizens as a matter of legal obligation. Such developments have not occurred in isolation, but rather alongside international trends in the post-WWII era. The brutal atrocities of the Holocaust in Europe created a reaction in world opinion strongly in favour of human rights protection. From the West and, in a more rhetorical way, from the Soviet-dominated East, calls came for protection of individual fundamental freedoms and liberties from state interference (civil and political rights), and promotion of the provision of the basic necessities of life to all, through state spending and regulation (social and economic rights). Recognition of some of these "basic" human rights is found in domestic constitutional guarantees and declarations, including the Canadian *Charter*, in a number of regional treaties and agreements, and in a variety of international instruments to which Canada is a signatory.[10] Taken together, developments in international law and the domestic laws of many states represent a significant pedigree of constitutional and human rights instruments, bolstering the claim that Canada, too, requires a constitutionalized scheme of social and economic rights.

There have been lone voices in the past calling for the entrenchment of social welfare rights. Activist and legal scholar Frank Scott, advocated that Canada entrench a Bill of Rights that included rights to basic necessities and work-place rights.[11] More recently, during the U.S.–Canada free trade debate there were calls for a social charter. Advocates argued that Canadian workers could not be expected to compete with workers in "right to work" states where union security rights are severely restricted. Nor could they compete more generally with wage labour in the U.S., given the lower rates of taxation and lower regulatory standards in some areas of that country. To level the playing field, it was argued, the United States would have to guarantee that certain social welfare measures be provided to American workers, as they are in Canada. These calls went largely unheeded, though they are once again being made in the context of NAFTA.[12]

Contemporary advocates of a social charter point to the increasing tendency of governments to withdraw from the provision of social welfare, and to the trends towards deregulation and privatization during the last fifteen years. The federal government, through its policy of budgetary restraint, has placed caps on contributions to social welfare programs that had previously been agreed to in cost-sharing arrangements with the provinces.[13] In harmony with Ottawa, provincial governments have been promoting fiscally conservative policies through the 1980s, focusing on deficit reduction at the expense of social spending. It is probably not too cynical to say that the war on poverty of the 1960s has given way to a war on social services in the 1980s and 1990s.[14] The rise of an "everybody is out for themselves" ideology is reflected in material conditions of deep poverty, unemployment and homelessness, and the reprivatization of social services through food banks, soup kitchens, and increasing reliance on private charity to fill the void left by the erosion of state obligations. In short, we have seen in the last fifteen years a material and ideological attack on the idea developed (albeit imperfectly realized) in the postwar period, that citizens are entitled as a matter of right to a measure of economic security and dignity. In this context, it is not surprising that the left has responded with the idea of a constitutional social charter – one that reflects a desire to place the all too vulnerable rights and obligations that constitute the Canadian social welfare state beyond the potentially destructive reach of governments.

Another important factor in the social charter story is that the demise of the social welfare state in Canada has been (and is) occurring at a time of severe constitutional instability, even crisis. The desire to make the 1982 constitutional amendments apply to Quebec led to a reopening of constitutional negotiations in 1987, and these culminated in the failure of the Meech Lake Accord. Two important strands of criticism can be identified in the debates that eventually led to that failure, each embodying a conception of citizenship that later played a role in the development of the social charter idea. The first criticism, embodying a conception of citizenship as inclusion, focused on the proposal's failure to include recognition of various sectors of Canadian society – women, First Nations, visible minorities, and so on. The proposals, it was argued, perpetuated the traditional racist and colonial understanding that the French and English were the two "founding nations" of Canada, and that the Constitution was only about their political relationship. Quebec was recognized as a distinct society, but other communities and collectivities were ignored. It was argued that their exclusion from the Constitution denied them the symbolic trappings of citizenship. Worse than that, the conferral of distinct society status on Quebec was perceived by some groups as potentially empowering Quebec to halt the exercise of these groups' collective aspirations. The second criticism was related to the Meech Lake Accord's spending-power proposal (one substantially reproduced in the Charlottetown Accord), and it embodied an understanding of Canadian citizenship that emphasized the importance of uniformity of social programs across the country. One of Quebec's central demands was (and is) to limit constitutionally the extent to which the federal government can spend, and thereby indirectly regulate, in areas within exclusive provincial jurisdiction. This was reflected in a provision of the Meech Lake Accord. People on the left feared the provision would lead to the constitutional Balkanization of the Canadian social welfare state. The left in Canada, and most quarters in the NDP, have generally favoured shared-cost programs. There was concern that the Meech Lake Accord's limitations on the federal government's role in the provision of social welfare would cause standards of social services and access to social services to vary across the country, undermining the shared commitment to social values central to Canadian citizenship.

These two criticisms of the Meech Lake Accord had considerable resonance among the public, and contributed to the ultimate demise of the Accord. Another round of constitutional negotiations followed, and it was here that Ontario's Premier Bob Rae saw an opportunity to proclaim and protect, through consti-tutional entrenchment of a social charter, cherished social programs such as universal medicare and education. The federal government at first expressed little interest in Ontario's social charter idea. Indeed, it is widely believed that the federal government proposed the inclusion of property rights in the *Charter* as a bargaining chip for the Ontario proposal: property rights would be bargained off the table if the social charter was too. However, the federal government needed the co-operation of the Premier of Ontario in order to achieve a constitutional accommodation, and it later warmed up to the proposition. This warmth was expressed at a series of constitutional conferences organized by the federal government as a back-up to the stalled Parliamentary Committee on the Constitution. As Harry Glasbeek argues in Chapter 8 of this volume, however, it was only after the proposal was embraced at the Montreal conference on the economic union that the social charter became a real possibility. The Ontario proposal only came to be understood fully through a series of documents released by the Ontario government. It was reasonably clear that it would not entitle citizens to go before courts to claim social rights; rather, the commitment would be largely inter-governmental, as are the current commitments respecting equalization of payments to the provinces in s. 36 of the *Constitution Act, 1982*. Indeed, as the proposal was clarified by the Ontario government and the federal New Democrats, the social charter was suggested to be in the form of an amendment to s.36. Further havoc at the Parliamentary Committee on the Constitution had the effect of shoring up the social charter. The Beaudoin-Dobbie Committee was required by law to report back to Parliament with its recommendations regarding constitutional reform by the end of February, 1992. As the final days drew closer, the possibility of a unanimous report, which was a critical objective of the federal government, became less likely. The conservative strategy was to split the NDP-Liberal alliance on the Committee by offering to New Democrats strong language in a new "social covenant". The covenant which subsequently emerged, with all-party support, bore the unmistakable stamp of the NDP, being similar to that in the Ontario government's original proposal.

For antipoverty activists, the proposed covenant was not suf-ficient protection for those living in conditions of poverty or for the continued existence of the social programs themselves. There emerged in response to the Ontario government proposal calls for a justiciable social charter which would permit those most reliant on the welfare state to claim not just entitlements, but rights, before courts of law. Many in the antipoverty community saw in the Ontario and Beaudoin-

Dobbie version a potential for making the situation worse by endangering the potential of the *Canadian Charter of Rights and Freedoms* to be interpreted in a manner which promoted social rights (see, for example, the papers by Brodsky and Nedelsky and Scott in this volume). In the interests of forging a stronger alliance in the antipoverty community, and also to make their proposal more attractive to governments, a Draft Social Charter, later becoming the Alternative Social Charter (ASC), was released by a coalition of antipoverty groups in March 1991. This proposal contained a dyad of enforcement mechanisms, but a very limited role for the courts. The Beaudoin-Dobbie version, and ultimately the Charlottetown Accord, while they endorse a monitoring mechanism rather than justiciability, do not provide any detail about how such a mechanism would work. That is to be discussed at some future First Ministers' meeting.

Throughout these various documents and the debates around them, the themes underlying the two major criticisms of the Meech Lake Accord are apparent. As discussed above, those themes can best be understood in terms of two concepts of citizenship – "citizenship as inclusion" and "citizenship as national standards". The citizenship as inclusion argument saw the major failing of the Accord in its exclusion, both in symbolic and real terms, of women, First Nations, and others. In the social charter context, this kind of argument is made about poor and disempowered people. The social charter is presented as a means of empowering, and including as citizens, the poor and disempowered in Canada. The argument portrays today's increasing poverty, malnutrition, homelessness and other social ills as denying their victims effective citizenship. Citizenship is understood here as meaning more than basic liberal democratic rights to liberty, formal equality and participation in elections. These provide only formal guarantees and do not allow for actual participation in social, economic and political life. The latter requires genuine protection of people's social and economic welfare, and this is why social rights to health care, an adequate standard of living, housing, and so on, are necessary. The exclusion of such rights from a constitution is tantamount to the exclusion of poor and disempowered people themselves; and this, in turn, denies them effective citizenship.[15]

Citizenship is also understood in the context of national standards in social charter discourse. The very meaning of *Canadian* citizenship – our national identity – is portrayed in this context as being wrapped up in the tradition of the caring and benevolent Canadian state where the harshness of capitalism is modified by government policy. In the first set of federal proposals following the failure of the Meech Lake Accord, the federal government talked about "our shared Canadian citizenship" as premised upon "a sense of shared values and commitments to our country."[16] These are the kinds of ideas that Premier Rae drew upon in first articulating the need for a social charter. In his view, a central feature of Canadian citizenship is the social welfare state that has developed in the postwar period and, for this reason, it should be in the Constitution: "Over time, the idea of Canadian citizenship has evolved and broadened.... Taken together, [major social] programs represent and symbolize Canadians' sense of themselves as members of a community where solidarity and mutual responsibility are fundamental social norms."[17] Similarly, the Beaudoin-Dobbie *Report* states: "Our intention in recommending a social covenant is to reinforce the [commitments to social programs currently expressed in the Constitution] and express other governmental commitments to social programs which Canadians see as part of their national identity."[18] As well, the *Report* says that "many people are deeply attached ... to national standards, seeing this as an essential part of Canadian citizenship."[19]

Arguably, the emphasis on citizenship concerns in relation to the Constitution can be understood, at least in part, as resulting from the entrenchment of the *Canadian Charter* in 1982. That document recognizes (albeit imperfectly) the identity and interests of groups previously not included in the constitutional framework – women, disabled people, racial and ethnic minorities, and First Nations, for example; as well, it establishes national (albeit elastic) standards for their protection. Placed beside the 1982 amendments, one can see why the Meech Lake Accord looked to many like a regressive step. It represented a return to the traditional view of constitutional law, one in which the Constitution is concerned only with the relationship between the federal government and the provinces.[20] The movement for a social charter can be understood as an attempt to extend and deepen the constitutional paradigm symbolized in the *Canadian Charter* and unsuccessfully challenged by the Meech Lake Accord. Here, a constitutional document is understood as reflecting and protecting, through rights, the needs, aspirations and identities of all groups in Canadian society, thus ensuring their full citizenship. For many social charter advocates, the *Canadian Charter* does not go far enough; its civil and political rights must be supplemented with social rights. Seen in this light, the social charter idea inevitably raises questions about the relationship between constitutional rights and progressive social change.

This question has been much considered in the context of the *Canadian Charter*.[21] A quite heated debate has developed among activists and academics on the utility of the *Canadian Charter*'s rights in advancing progressive social struggle. On one side of the debate, a number of arguments are made in support of the position that constitutional rights are either useless, or positively dangerous, in the development and success of social struggles. First, it is argued that constitutional rights to liberty and equality may sound good in the abstract, but the judiciary is unlikely to give them progressive content because of the conservative attitudes and beliefs of most judges. Second, critics of rights argue that even if courts could be relied upon to give rights progressive content, the cost of litigation is simply too great for anybody but the very wealthy to pursue remedies for rights violations. Next, it is argued that the form of constitutional rights precludes their being put to progressive use. Such rights tend to be libertarian in form, providing individuals with protection from state coercion but leaving untouched the unequal social relations in which they live. Scholars have pointed to the irony that rights discourse protects individuals from the state, when it is the state, through social programs and regulation, that protects individuals from the more egregious forms of social inequality, exploitation and suffering that might otherwise be the result of market relations. Finally, critical scholars are concerned that rights discourse legalizes social issues outside as well as inside the courts, reformulating them in abstract and individualist terms to the detriment of progressive politics.

On the other side of the debate, defenders of rights argue for a more positive conception of rights. To begin with, they point out, while judges might be conservative, so too are officials in various other state agencies; judicial conservatism is but an example of the more general conservativism of state personnel, not a special case. Similarly, the argument about litigation being expensive can equally well be made about lobbying of government agencies. Thus, neither arguments about judicial personnel nor arguments about access to justice demonstrate that rights litigation is necessarily any worse than other forms of political claims available to progressive groups. Nor are supporters of rights strategies moved by arguments that point to the limiting effects of the form of rights, either within the courts or in political discourse more generally. To begin with, they point out that protection *from* the state is not at all unimportant for progressive struggles, especially at a time when state authoritarianism, usually under the guise of law and order, is on the rise. Second, they argue, abstraction, individualism and antistatism are not necessarily formal attributes of rights; the concept of rights can be, and has been, understood in collectivist, social and positive terms, making rights an important strategy for those involved in social struggles. When it comes to the role of rights discourse outside the courts, in political discourse, supporters of rights argue that the availability of rights discourse is important for motivating, organizing and mobilizing groups involved in social struggle.

The social charter idea meets some of the concerns of those who are critical of rights. In all proposals, for example, the rights and commitments articulated impose positive obligations on the state, thus avoiding the libertarian form of civil and political rights. For advocates of rights strategies, the social charter idea provides a potential deepening of rights resources and is another arena of struggle for social change. However, as the following essays demonstrate, rights critics still find much to be critical about in relation to the social charter idea and proposals; and rights advocates are concerned that the Charlottetown Accord's social union clause did not go far enough. A common goal of all the authors in this volume is the advancement of social justice and progressive change, but this shared commitment does not necessarily translate into support of the social charter idea, nor the Charlottetown Accord's social union provision. To the contrary, the kind of debate and insights about the relationship between rights and social change that has taken place in relation to the *Canadian Charter* is now developed in the context of proposals for a social charter or union. The authors whose essays are collected here look at the rights debate, in the social charter context, from a variety of vantage points.

For Martha Jackman, the social charter debate has been hampered by an unwillingness, particularly on the left, to argue in favour of justiciable social rights. She takes up this issue by responding to the common critiques of justiciable rights. She argues that the distinction between classical political rights and social rights has been overplayed, and that rights litigation is a legitimate and effective strategy for achieving social change. Why privilege the legislative process, she asks, and thus foreclose one of few alternative forums available to the disadvantaged, particularly when powerful forces in society have access to both legislative and judicial forums? For Jackman, the non-justiciable social union clause represents a lost opportunity to develop a fuller notion of Canadian citizenship. Lucie Lamarche, too, sees the social union clause as a lost opportunity to enhance rights protection for the socially and economically disadvantaged. She points out that the *Canadian Charter of Rights and Freedoms* does not recognize adequately those social and economic rights which Canada has pledged to protect in a variety of international human rights instruments. Even when Charter jurisprudence occupies itself with these concerns, the courts have exhibited a startling degree of deference to legislative choices in the social policy arena. Like Martha Jackman, Lucie Lamarche argues for a fully justiciable social charter which does not segregate social rights from political rights. For Lamarche, the social union clause has less to do with rights than with the financing of federal commitments under renewed federalism.

Gwen Brodsky agrees with Lamarche that the Charter jurisprudence to date fails to protect the interests of the poor. However, she considers that this has more to do with the inadequacies of the judiciary rather than deficiencies in the *Charter*. Generously inter-preted, in her view, the *Charter* could provide important protections for poor people. Indeed, she is concerned that a social charter might actually undermine the *Canadian Charter*'s potential to advance social justice. Brodsky's view that the courts have not done a good job with the *Charter* underlines her support of a *non*-justiciable social charter. In place of judicial application, she prescribes a monitoring agency that would be empowered to review governments' performance with social programs and also hear complaints from aggrieved individuals and groups. Essentially, Brodsky endorses the Alternative Social Charter model advanced by a coalition of anti-poverty groups in March 1992. That model is endorsed as well by Jennifer Nedelsky and Craig Scott, who describe and defend the Alternative Social Charter and place it in a philosophical context. They share many of the concerns of the rights critics about using social rights to advance social justice. But they see in the social charter an opportunity to engage in meaningful dialogue about the social conditions of the disadvantaged. They consider that rights are best understood as structuring relationships, and a social charter could move the discussion about those relationships forward. They argue in favour of the ASC's monitoring and enforcement mechanism which would, in their view, institutionalize and provide an ongoing site for social rights dialogue.

A number of the authors in this collection go beyond a critique of the Charlottetown Accord's social union proposal, and criticize the idea of a social charter more generally. For them, using constitutional rights to advance social justice is an ineffective and possibly even dangerous strategy. Joel Bakan develops this kind of argument, pointing out that the effect of social rights will depend upon how they are interpreted by whomever is charged with their enforcement. Accordingly, he argues, progressive results are not guaranteed, and regressive ones are possible; moreover, if governments are forced to redirect spending in order to satisfy an order under the social charter, this could lead to the paring down of other social programs. Bakan goes further to address an issue often taken for granted in the social charter debate; that is, the desirable symbolic effect of entrenching social rights in the Constitution. He sees the social charter as entrenching an incomplete vision of citizenship, one which is concerned solely with treating social ills rather than eliminating their causes. Hester Lessard is concerned too with the symbolism that the social charter represents. For her, it is the symbolism of the social contract, reinforcing the current map of political and economic power, the public-private split, and the apparent neutrality of the state. She explores the use of contract language in constitutional discussions, a language embedded in relationships of domination and subordination. By entrenching this new social contract, Lessard says, we bury further the existing state of social services into the realm of normalcy and naturalness, and for women who are seeking control over their reproductive lives, the social charter represents the further retrenchment of a contract which continues to subordinate women's experiences.

In line with Bakan and Lessard, Harry Glasbeek is suspicious of the social charter idea and its alleged benefits. He situates the debate in the context of current political and economic restructuring in Canada. As was to be expected, he argues, social charter advocates were not accorded a fully justiciable social charter which could trump the individualist hierarchy entrenched in the *Canadian Charter of Rights and Freedoms*. Moreover, the social charter was simply a card to be played against Progressive Conservative pressures to constitutionalize further the free market, via proposals to entrench the common market and a right to property. Glasbeek advocates that those fighting for social justice do so where it counts the most, and where social rights actually can be achieved: through direct legislative action. David Schneiderman also addresses the political economic dimensions of the social charter debate. After the demise of the Meech Lake Accord and the emergence of the "Canada round" of negotiations, he points out, there were openings for alternative constitutional visions to appear. It was the social charter which emerged to fill this void. Yet, social charter advocates failed to address the underlying crisis in the funding of the welfare state which precipitated discussion about the social charter in the first place. He concludes that the left has failed to take full advantage of the opening provided in this constitutional round of discussion, leaving the terrain of political economy entirely to fiscal conservatives.

Finally, Glenn Drover situates the social charter debate within the discourse of social philosophy, and so provides a larger context for the preceding discussion. As do other authors, he explores the distinction between positive and negative rights and also examines the European experience with social rights, both within social charters and in constitutions. But he goes further to distinguish between general and specific egalitarianism. The former tenders rationales for the recognition of social welfare rights, the latter postulates what those rights might constitute in practice. Those specific entitlements are then tested against communitarian and feminist critiques, and Drover concludes in the end that social minima, as articulated in social charter proposals, do not meet concerns about justice and welfare raised by these critiques.

Endnotes

[1] See T.H. Marshall, "Citizenship and Social Class" in *Class, Citizenship and Social Development* (New York: Anchor Books, 1965).

[2] A. Moscovitch and G. Drover "Inequality and Social Welfare" in Moscovitch and Drover, eds., *Inequality: Essays on the Political Economy of Social Welfare* (Toronto: University of Toronto Press, 1981).

3   See Frank Strain and Derek Hum, "Canadian Federalism and the Welfare State: Shifting Responsibilities and Sharing Costs" in Jacqueline S. Israel, ed., *The Canadian Welfare State: Evolution and Transition* (Edmonton: The University of Alberta Press, 1987) at 354.

4   This is discussed in D.V. Smiley, ed., *The Rowell-Sirois Report, Book 1* (Toronto: MacMillan, 1978) at 174ff.

5   See *Re Weekly Rest in Industrial Undertakings Act, Minimum Wages Act and Limitation of Hours Act*, [1937] 1 D.L.R. 673; *Re Employment and Social Insurance Act*, [1937] 1 D.L.R. 684; *Re Dominion Trade and Commission Act*, [1937] 1 D.L.R. 702.

6   Moscovitch and Drover, *supra*, note 2.

7   *Ibid.*

8   *Ibid.*

9   *Ibid.*

10 See Ontario Ministry of Attorney General, Constitutional Law and Policy Division, *The Protection of Social and Economic Rights: A Comparative Study*, (Toronto: Ministry of Attorney General, 1991).

11 See Frank R. Scott, *What Does Labour Need in a Bill of Rights?* (Halifax: Institute of Public Affairs, 1959).

12 See Matthew Sanger, *Free Trade and Worker's Rights: The European Social Charter* (Ottawa: Canadian Centre for Policy Alternatives, May 1991).

13 See *Government Expenditures Restraint Act* , S.C. 1991, c.9.

14 Michael Katz, *The Undeserving Poor: From the War on Poverty to the War on Welfare* (New York: Pantheon Books, 1989).

15 See Bryan Turner, *Citizenship and Capitalism: The Debate Over Reformism* (London: Allen & Unwin, 1986); P. Macklem and C. Scott, "Constitutional Ropes of Sand or Justiciable Guarantees? Social Rights in a New South African Constitution"(1992) 141 U. Pennsylvania Law Rev. [forthcoming].

16 *Shaping Canada's Future Together* (Ottawa: Minister of Supply and Services, 1991) at 1-2.

17 Ontario, Ministry of Intergovernmental Affairs, *A Canadian Social Charter: Making Our Shared Values Stronger* (Toronto: Ministry of Intergovernmental Affairs, 1991) at 2.

18 Special Joint Committee on a Renewed Canada, *A Renewed Canada: The Report of the Special Joint Committee of the Senate and the House of Commons*, (Ottawa: Queen's Printer, 1992).

19 *Ibid.* at 64.

20 J. Bakan and D. Pinard, Getting to the Bottom of Meech Lake (1989) 21 Ottawa L. Rev. 247.

[21] See, for recent examples, J. Bakan, "Constitutional Interpretation and Social Change: You Can't Always Get What You Want (Nor What You Need)" (1991) 70 Can. Bar Rev. 307; Amy Bartholemew and Alan Hunt "What's Wrong with Rights" (1990) 9 *Law and Inequality* 1; Judy Fudge and Harry Glasbeek, "The Politics of Rights: A Politics with Little Class" (1992) 1 *Social and Legal Studies* 45.

2

Constitutional Rhetoric and Social Justice: Reflections on the Justiciability Debate*

Martha Jackman

Introduction

In a climate of general economic insecurity and in view of recent federal policies relating to unemployment insurance, intergovernmental transfers, and continental free trade, among other matters, it is not surprising that the idea of a social charter has attracted significant public interest and support. The Ontario government's initial efforts to put a social charter on the constitutional reform agenda, and Premier Rae's release of a discussion paper on the subject in September 1991[1] were welcomed by poverty rights advocates across Canada, who lamented the absence of explicit reference to social rights in the 1982 *Canadian Charter of Rights and Freedoms*. The optimism generated by the emergence of the social charter as a constitutional reform issue has, however, been short lived. No government – NDP or otherwise – seems prepared to support the entrenchment of anything stronger than a declaration of good intentions. In an interview relating to the Beaudoin-Dobbie Committee *Report*,[2] Toronto housing rights activist Bruce Porter commented that "[a] weak social charter could be worse than no charter at all."[3] Porter's remarks reflected growing concerns in the antipoverty and equality-seeking communities that the socially and economically disadvantaged may in fact be worse off as a result of the social charter initiative.[4]

The Ontario government discussion paper on the social charter canvassed a number of options. These included strengthening existing constitutional commitments to equalization and the reduction of interregional disparities; expanding the welfare component of the interprovincial mobility rights clause under section 6 of the *Canadian Charter of Rights and Freedoms*; entrenching a general statement of principles which would inform social and economic policy making; and adding certain basic and justiciable social rights to the constitution. The official proposals released by the Ontario government in February 1992 were, however, disappointingly modest.[5] The government opted for an expanded version of the non-justiciable principles set out in section 36 of the *Constitution Act, 1982*, abandoning any mention of justiciable individual rights to specific programs or services.

In its proposals for a new "social covenant," released at the end of February 1992, the Beaudoin-Dobbie Committee also rejected the idea of a justiciable social charter in favour of a largely declaratory one. The Committee recommended that a new section 36.1 be added to the constitution, one "which would commit governments to fostering" a number of "social commitments," including comprehensive, universal, portable, publicly administered and accessible health care; adequate social services and social benefits; high quality education; the rights of workers to organize and bargain collectively; and the integrity of the environment. The Committee explained its preference for a social covenant framed in terms of constitutional commitments, rather than justiciable social rights, on the grounds that:

> While these commitments are in many ways as important to Canadians as their legal rights and freedoms, they are different. These commitments express goals, not rights and they embrace responsibilities of enormous scope.

Therefore, while these are appropriate subjects for constitutional recognition, elected governments should retain the
authority to decide how they can best be fulfilled. We
believe that the matters addressed in the Social Covenant
are best resolved through democratic means.[6]

The Committee acknowledged, however, that in order for the commitments contained in the covenant to "be more than merely words,"
governmental compliance must be subject to some form of public
review. The Committee recommended that this review be carried
out by a specialized commission, which would hold public hearings
and table periodic reports in Parliament and in provincial and territorial legislatures. The proposals which emerged in the Charlottetown
Accord[7] of August 28, 1992 provided for the entrenchment, under
section 36.1 of the *Constitution Act, 1982*, of a new social and economic union clause, which set out the federal and provincial
governments' commitment to the "principle of the preservation and
development of Canada's social and economic union." This commitment would be expressed through a series of non-justiciable "policy
objectives" relating to health care, social services and benefits, and
education, among other matters. The Charlottetown Accord recommended that a First Ministers' Conference should determine a
mechanism for monitoring the social and economic union. It also
recommended that a provision clarifying the relationship between
the new clause and the exisiting *Charter* should be drafted, and that a
clause should be added to the Constitution stating that the social and
economic union does not "abrogate or derogate" from the *Charter*.

The Case against Justiciability

The unwillingness reflected in the Ontario government proposal, the
Beaudoin-Dobbie *Report*, and the Charlottetown Accord to support a
social charter containing justiciable social rights is shared by many
constitutional scholars and others on the left. Criticism is based on
three main arguments. First, social rights should be distinguished
from more traditional civil and political guarantees for purposes of
constitutional recognition. Second, courts are an inappropriate forum for resolving the complex social, political and resource allocation
issues which would be raised by social rights claims. And third, the
pursuit of rights is in itself suspect as a mechanism for social change.

The remainder of the paper will describe and respond to these arguments. The paper will conclude that a social charter which fails to include basic and justiciable social rights may indeed be worse than no social charter at all.

The distinction between classical and social rights

The first argument against the entrenchment of justiciable social rights is based on perceived distinctions between classical and social rights, and their appropriateness as a matter for judicial review.[8] Classical, or "negative" rights, it is argued, reflect natural and inherent traits in human beings. In order for these traits to become rights, the state need only recognize their existence and refrain from interfering with them. Social or "positive" rights, on the other hand, do not come into existence automatically upon their recognition. Rather, the state must act affirmatively to create them or to ensure the conditions necessary for their enjoyment. And, while the content of classical rights is seen as relatively universal and precise, social rights are considered highly subjective and imprecise in character.

These differences have significant implications for the role of the judiciary. To respond to a complaint brought by an individual whose classical or negative rights have been infringed, the court need only invalidate the state action causing the interference and, if necessary, order the state to refrain from further action. As a result, it is argued, judicial enforcement of negative rights imposes minimal financial or administrative burdens on the state. To vindicate a claim for social rights, however, the court may have to order the state to act affirmatively, in some more or less specific way. Such judicial remedies will often require substantial and long-term state intervention and expenditure. Because of the contingent nature of social rights, and the lack of objective standards in this area, many fear that judges deciding social rights claims will substitute their own values for those of democratically elected, and accountable, legislatures. In enforcing social rights, courts will effectively engage in social policy making, forcing governments to expend public funds in ways they did not plan or choose. In addition to eroding public confidence in the independence and integrity of the judiciary, it is claimed that this usurpation of policy making by the courts will lead to an abdication of responsibility by governments, and to frustration and eventual apathy in voters. In short, judicial enforcement of social rights, by transferring control over social and economic policy making from elected legislatures to unelected and unaccountable courts, is seen as inconsistent with basic democratic principles and therefore highly undesirable.

Social rights and judicial competence

A second set of arguments against justiciable social rights suggests that courts are institutionally incompetent to deal with the complex social, political and resource allocation issues which would inevitably be raised by individual social rights claims.[9] For a number of reasons, including the complexity of judicial procedures, the incomprehensibility of judicial language, the formality and adversarial nature of judicial process, and the prohibitive cost of litigation, courts are virtually inaccessible to the poor. Also, because of the narrow socio-economic, racial and cultural backgrounds from which they are drawn, their generally close prior ties with the business community, and their highly specialized education, training and expertise, judges are ill-suited and ill-disposed to the task of interpreting and applying social rights. Courts face additional constraints at informational and remedial levels. Courts do not control their own agendas, but must deal with specific matters brought before them by individual litigants in the context of individual disputes, within the restrictive bounds of judicial procedure. Unlike governments, which have wide discretion in deciding when and how to act, courts are limited in the range of factors which they can take into account in resolving disputes; they are precluded from devising complex solutions to complex problems; and their enforcement powers are limited.

These limitations are particularly relevant in relation to social rights, since by definition these must be interpreted and applied in a very contextual way. Courts must have access to the information necessary for them to decide what the scope and content of a given social right should be. In remedying social rights violations, courts will potentially be required to tell governments what benefits or services they must provide, and in what quality or quantity. Such determinations require a thorough grasp of social and economic conditions in the society, as well as knowledge of public perceptions of the community's needs and means. Legislatures, and not courts, it is argued, are in the best position to make the complex judgments which these questions require.

The pursuit of rights as a mechanism for social change

A final objection to justiciable social rights reflects broader concerns relating to rights-seeking as a form of social action and as a mechanism for social change.[10] In one variant of the critique, the pursuit of rights is seen as a new and damaging social trend which pits individualistic American-style conceptions of citizenship against traditional Canadian collectivist visions of the relationship between individual, community, and the state. In this conception, the individual as bearer of rights is seen as an incomplete and flawed construction of personhood, or as one commentator describes it, "an emaciated, juridical conception of ourselves."[11]

More prominent in legal critiques of rights and rights-seeking is the argument that the constitutional entrenchment of rights represents a "liberal lie," promoting a false expectation in disadvantaged individuals and groups that the pursuit of legal rights through the courts can effect lasting social change, or that formal recognition of rights can have any real transformative impact on underlying social institutions, values, and conditions. Rights, it is claimed, operate instead to perpetuate existing power structures in society, and to channel potentially radical demands for change into legal claims which, by definition, will not be disruptive of the social and economic *status quo*.

An Assessment of the Social Rights Critique

Viewed from the perspective of the socially and economically disadvantaged, rejection by the Ontario government and the Beaudoin-Dobbie Committee, and in the Charlottetown Accord of justiciable social rights, and the arguments upon which this rejection is based, present serious difficulties. In its present form, the *Canadian Charter of Rights and Freedoms* grants individuals a range of rights: the rights to conscience and religion, thought and expression, assembly and association, fair trial, and equality, among others. Because these rights are included in the category of classical or negative rights, their justiciability is rarely questioned. The distinction between negative and positive rights is, however, open to serious challenge.[12] Once one moves beyond the most personal of human rights – such as the right to freedom of conscience or belief – the arguments that classical rights reflect natural and inherent traits in human beings, that they are absolute in character, or that their recognition imposes negligible costs on the state, are hard to sustain.

Many classical rights, such as the right to vote, the right to fair trial, and the rights to freedom of expression and association, do not come into existence automatically upon their recognition; rather, they are dependent on concerted state regulation and action, not on any absence of state compulsion or control. It is therefore simplistic to suggest that recognition and respect for classical rights imposes only negligible costs on the state. In most cases the state is attempting to pursue some competing public interest when it violates a constitutional right. When such an activity is found unconstitutional, the state must find some alternate means of achieving the same purposes. And classical rights which require affirmative state action for their enjoyment clearly involve corresponding financial and administrative costs. The distinction based on the universality of classical rights and the indeterminacy of social rights is also one of degree rather than one of kind. To say that a classical right, such as freedom of expression or the right to fair trial, is universal surely means no more than that it is recognized in many societies, and not that its content is static across cultures and across time.

It is important to realize that traditional distinctions between classical or negative rights, and social or positive rights, and the willingness to provide for judicial enforcement of one but not the other, operate in fact to discriminate against the poor. To be in a position to complain about state interferences with rights, one has to exercise and enjoy them. But without access to adequate food, clothing, income, education, housing and medical care, it is impossible to benefit from most traditional human rights guarantees. It requires little imagination to question the value and meaning of a right to freedom of conscience and opinion without adequate food; to freedom of expression without adequate education; to security of the person without adequate shelter and health care. In each case there exists a fundamental interdependence between the classical right, which is constitutionally recognized, and the underlying social right which is assumed to be a matter not for the state but for the market, for individual initiative, or even for nature.

From the perspective of the disadvantaged, arguments relating to democracy and judicial legitimacy must also be reassessed. The insistence that courts are incompetent to engage in social policy making ignores their historic and continuing intervention in this area. Courts create social policy not only in their interpretation of the *Canadian Charter of Rights and Freedoms*, but also in interpreting federal and provincial economic, labour, environmental and other legislation, as well as in their resolution of private law disputes. More significantly, the claim that the entrenchment of justiciable social rights is antidemocratic conflates Parliamentary representation with democracy itself. This is particularly problematic given that many of the decisions which bear most heavily on the welfare of the poor are made not by Parliament, but by other government actors within Cabinet, government departments and administrative agencies, over whom Parliament exercises very little control. The view that justiciable social rights are inimical to democracy fails to recognize the role of the courts as an avenue for challenges to the antidemocratic behaviour of Parliament and its delegates. It also fails to consider the extent to which social rights can, by expanding the number of participants and the quality of participation, enhance democratic decision making by elected governments and other public institutions.[13]

Critiques of rights-seeking must also be re-examined.[14] The argument that meaningful social change cannot be achieved through the pursuit of legal rights suggests that the judiciary is somehow distinct from ordinary politics and government, and that legal institutions, legal reasoning, and litigation are not legitimate arenas for social action and debate. By failing to accept judicial challenges and rights-seeking as legitimate strategies for reform, the anti-rights critique recreates the dichotomy, challenged by progressive lawyers since the 1920s, between politics and law.

To the ears of the disadvantaged, the argument that Canada is becoming "Charterized," that rights-bearing is a truncated form of personhood, or that the politics of rights is antidemocratic, also ring hollow. These arguments ignore the fact that, for many disadvantaged Canadians, social citizenship and political efficacy are not universal traits but are socially constituted and controlled. To the extent that the politics of rights has pushed legislatures to expand access to the political process and to remove other barriers to full social citizenship, the dismissal of rights-bearing as an element of personhood, and of rights-seeking as a component of democracy, is a serious error. In short, the suggestion that social rights should be insulated from the courts and left to the legislatures ignores the realities of the Canadian political process. The view that judicial review threatens democratic values rests on the premise that the political process is functioning properly, and that the courts should therefore defer to popularly elected governments on matters of fundamental social policy. From the perspective of the disadvantaged, however, there is no reason to spurn the intervention of the courts in social policy making, since that intervention will frequently increase their ability to influence the legislative and policy processes, and to call legislatures to account for their decisions.

While the socially and economically disadvantaged may not be adequately represented by the courts, neither are they well represented by other branches of government. If judicial representation and access are a real concern, reforms of the judicial appointments process and judicial procedure are a more effective response than excluding the claims of the disadvantaged from the courts. And, even allowing that the economically disadvantaged have better access to legislatures than to courts, it is hard to understand why they should be restricted to one forum, when the economically advantaged in Canada have always had ample access to both.

Conclusion

There is a further reason for rejecting the declaratory model proposed by the Ontario government and the Beaudoin-Dobbie Committee and reflected in the Charlottetown Accord, and further reason for insisting that fundamental social rights be justiciable in the same way as the more traditional civil and political rights already contained in the *Canadian Charter of Rights and Freedoms*. As many have argued, a constitution is more than a legal document. It is a highly symbolic and ideologically significant one – reflecting both who we are as a society, and who we would like to be. Inclusion of certain rights and principles in the constitution says a great deal about their stature and importance; omission of others has the same effect. A decision to entrench a weak social charter which does not include basic justiciable social rights confirms the view that social rights are different (by definition lesser) than the rights and freedoms the *Canadian Charter of Rights and Freedoms* already contains. Such a decision gives formal expression to the heretofore

implicit assumption that where one class of rights merits full constitutional recognition and respect, another more basic class of rights,
and their beneficiaries, do not.

Of immediate concern is the prospect that adoption of a non-
justiciable social charter may exacerbate the difficulties faced by those
individuals and groups now attempting to convince the courts that
the socially and economically disadvantaged are entitled to full enjoyment of the guarantees which the *Canadian Charter of Rights and
Freedoms* already contains, most notably the right to life, liberty and
security of the person under section 7, and the right to equal benefit
and equal protection of the law under section 15.[15] The emphasis in
the Beaudoin-Dobbie *Report,* and in other governmental statements
leading up to the Charlottetown Accord, on the proper division of
authority between the legislatures and the courts on matters of social
policy may diminish the rights of those facing social and economic
disadvantage, by encouraging the courts to refrain altogether from
reviewing governmental decisions relating to the allocation of social
programs and benefits, even where such decisions are clearly unconstitutional. Of concern in the longer term is the truncated
constitutional vision of Canada which the proposals contained in the
Charlottetown Accord reinforce. It has often been remarked that the
Canadian Charter of Rights and Freedoms is more reminiscent of a rights
document from the nineteenth century than the twentieth century.
This assessment is based on its failure to recognize the basic social
rights, such as the right to food, shelter, health care, education and
an adequate income, which are contained in most modern constitutions, and which are well established in international human rights
law. To many, this is all the more surprising given Canada's ratification in 1978 of the *International Covenant on Economic Social and Cultural
Rights,* and the country's longstanding social welfare traditions.

By rejecting the justiciability of basic and fundamental social
rights, Canada's First Ministers have lost a precious opportunity to
bring the *Canadian Charter of Rights and Freedoms* into the twentieth
century, and to transform it into a more faithful reflection of the
social values and aspirations which the vast majority of Canadians
share. By adopting an outmoded conception of rights, the
Charlottetown Accord proposals limited the Constitution's potential
for enhancing democracy. And by ignoring the fundamental interdependence between classical and social rights, the proposals ensured

that many Canadians will continue to be denied effective enjoyment of both. Thus, where the social and economic union has been discussed in terms of promoting "the goals of social well-being which are part of being Canadian," and reinforcing commitments to "social programs which are central to the idea of Canadian citizenship," the sound is more of constitutional rhetoric than it is of social justice.

Endnotes

* An earlier version of this paper appeared in the April 1992 issue of *Canadian Forum* and in Volume 1 of *Inroads*. Many of the ideas expressed are developed in greater depth in M. Jackman, "The Protection of Welfare Rights Under the Charter" (1988) 20 Ottawa L. Rev. 257.

1 Ontario, *A Canadian Social Charter - Making Our Shared Values Stronger* (Toronto: Ministry of Intergovernmental Affairs, September 1991).

2 Special Joint Committee of the Senate and the House of Commons on a Renewed Canada, *Report* (Ottawa: Queen's Printer, February 1992) (Co-chairs: G.-A. Beaudoin & D. Dobbie).

3 G. York, "Constitution's `social covenant' criticized for shortcomings" *The [Toronto] Globe & Mail* (9 March 1992) A4.

4 See for example, National Anti-Poverty Organization, Press Release, "Alternative Social Charter Proposed by Groups Across Canada" (27 March 1992), reproduced in Appendix I.

5 Ontario, Office of the Premier, News Release, "Ontario's Proposal for a Social Charter for Canada" (13 February 1992), reproduced in Appendix II.

6 Special Joint Committee on a Renewed Canada, *Report, supra,* note 2 at 88 and see Appendix III.

7 *Consensus Report on the Constitution* (Ottawa: Canadian Intergovernmental Conference, August 1992) and Appendix IV.

8 See for example W.S. Tarnopolsky, "The Equality Rights" in W.S. Tarnopolsky & G.-A. Beaudoin, eds, *The Canadian Charter Rights and Freedoms: Commentary* (Toronto: Carswell, 1982) at 438-39; P. Monahan, *Politics and the Constitution - The Charter, Federalism and the Supreme Court of Canada* (Toronto: Carswell/Methuen, 1987) at 126-27; D. Proulx, «La portée de la Charte canadienne des droits et libertés en matière de droits sociaux et collectifs» in *La Charte canadienne des droits et libertés et les droits collectifs et sociaux* (Trois Rivières: Université de Québec à Trois Rivières, 1983) 55.

9 See for example J. Frémont, «Les tribunaux et la *Charte*: le pouvoir d'ordonner la dépense de fonds publics en matières sociales et économiques» (1991) 36 McGill L.J. 1323; A. Petter, "The Politics of the

Charter" (1986) 8 Sup. Ct L. Rev 473; D.A. Schmeiser, "The Case Against the Entrenchment of a Canadian Bill of Rights" (1973) 1 Dalhousie L.J. 15.

[10] See for example R.I. Cheffins & P.A. Johnson, *The Revised Canadian Constitution - Politics as Law* (Toronto: McGraw-Hill Ryerson, 1986); A.C. Hutchinson & A. Petter, "Private Rights/Public Wrongs: The Liberal Lie of the Charter" (1988) 38 U.T.L.J. 278; J. Bakan, "Constitutional Interpretation and Social Change: You Can't Always Get What You Want (Nor What You Need)" (1991) 70 Can. Bar Rev. 307.

[11] T.C. Pocklington, "Some Drawbacks of the Politics of Constitutional Rights" (Winter 1991) 2 Constit. Forum 42 at 43.

[12] For an expanded critique of the distinction between positive and negative rights, see for example C.M. MacMillan, "Social versus Political Rights" (1986) 19 Can. J. Pol. Sci. 283; C. Scott & P. Macklem, "Constitutional Ropes of Sand or Justiciable Guarantees? Social Rights in a New South Africa Constitution" (1992) 141 U. Pennsylvania Law Rev. [forthcoming].

[13] For a discussion of this issue in the context of the existing *Charter*, see M. Jackman, "Rights and Participation: The Use of the Charter to Supervise the Regulatory Process" (1991) 4 C.J.A.L.P. 23.

[14] For an assessment of the rights critique in the Canadian context, see A. Bartholomew & S. Boyd, "Towards a Political Economy of Law" in W. Clement & G. Williams, *The New Canadian Political Economy* (Montreal: McGill-Queen's University Press, 1989) 212; H. Echenberg & B. Porter, "Poverty Stops Equality: Equality Stops Poverty - the Case for Social and Economic Rights" in R.I. Cholewinski, ed., *Human Rights in Canada* (Ottawa: Human Rights Research and Education Centre, 1990) 1.

[15] For a description of some of the poverty related *Charter* challenges currently under way, see *Status Report on Case Development and Litigation Supported by the Charter Committee on Poverty Issues* (Ottawa: National Anti-Poverty Organization, n.d.).

3

Le débat sur les droits sociaux au Canada: respecte-t-il la juridicité de ces droits?

Lucie Lamarche

On hésite encore trop souvent à prendre acte de la juridicité des droits économiques et sociaux. Cette réserve, somme toute, est tout autant politique que les causes mêmes de la segmentation historique entre les droits civils et politiques et les droits économiques et sociaux. Après avoir brièvement exposé les pièges de la segmentation des droits et ànoncé comment la Charte canadienne des droits participe à sa façon au processus de dénaturation des droits économiques et sociaux et à celui du renforcement des droits individuels, nous nous pencherons sur les pièges que recèlent l'actualisation du fédéralisme canadien en l'espèce pour nous attarder ensuite aux conceptualisations possibles de la constitutionalisation des droits économiques et sociaux et aux arguments le plus souvent invoqués contre un tel enchèssement. Un bref renvoi infrapaginal à la situation québécoise permettra d'illustrer que la simple ànonciation de tels droits ne constitue pas le

fin mot de l'histoire. Il va de soi que la brièveté du présent
commentaire nous contraint à un examen sommaire des objectifs
ànoncés ici.

Le piége de la segmentation des droits

On oublie trop souvent qu'à l'origine, les Pactes des Nations Unies
relatifs aux droits civils, politiques, économiques, sociaux et culturels
constituaient un Pacte unique[1] et que le droit à l'égalité est un droit
déterminant de l'exercice de l'ensemble de ces droits.[2] La Décennie
'80 a fourni aux Nations Unies de multiples occasions d'affirmer la
valeur équipollente de l'ensemble des droits de la personne et leur
réelle interdépendance.[3] De plus en plus, le Comité des droits de
l'homme et le Comité des droits économiques, sociaux et culturels
des Nations Unies reconnaissent tous deux leur juridiction incidente
sur l'un et l'autre des ensembles de droits. Ainsi, les droits à la dignité,
à la vie, au maintien de conditions d'existence décentes et suffisantes
existent en eux-mêmes et en relation d'interdépendance avec les autres
droits de la personne.

En droit international des personnes, la question de la *nature
juridique* des droits sociaux et économiques est devenue obsolète. Les
confusions entretenues entre la juridicisation[4] de ces droits et leur
justiciabilité[5] tiennent plutôt à la structure organique du *Pacte relatif
aux droits économiques, sociaux et culturels*, à la trop jeune existence du
Comité des droits économiques, sociaux et culturels[6] et au succès de
la stratégie d'évitement élaborée par les états parties aux Pactes en ce
qui concerne le respect des engagements relatifs aux droits
économiques et sociaux. Par conséquent, l'efficience actuelle des droits
sociaux et économiques sur la scene internationale, si relative soit-
elle, nous semble dériver essentiellement d'une extension de l'objet
des droits civils et politiques.[7] Ce constat doit aussi être jumelé à une
autre réalité à celle de l'émergence des droits dits de troisième
génération, lesquels, contrairement aux droits sociaux et économiques,
ont peut-être fait l'objet d'une juridicisation accélérée au détriment
de la crédibilité générale de l'ensemble des droits de deuxième et
troisième génération.[8]

On s'entend aujourd'hui pour admettre qu'au-delà de la question de leur énonciation en droit national, les droits sociaux et
économiques, ont été à tort pris pour acquis, au sein des économies

développées. La présence de cet apparent *magma* de droits mène, sur les scènes du droit national qui n'ont pas de tradition constitutionnelle en ce qui concerne l'énonciation de droits économiques et sociaux, à un rapport dialectique confus entre les droits civils et politiques énoncés et les *autres* droits et ce, sans égard aux multiples fonctions juridiques et politiques potentielles de l'énonciation des droits économiques et sociaux.

Au Canada, le *droit social* est livré aux aléas d'une Charte, qui, au-delà de ses fonctions récupératrices,[9] n'a jamais été élaborée, même dans ses tenants et aboutissants les plus implicites, en fonction des droits économiques et sociaux. Ainsi, les tentatives de faire reconnaître une certaine subjectivisation constitutionnelle des droits économiques et sociaux, si dérivée soit-elle, se sont avérées grandement insatisfaisantes à ce jour. Il n'est donc pas surprenant que devant une telle réalité, plusieurs groupes communautaires du Canada, constatant les limites et l'effet d'individualisation de la *Charte canadienne des droits* aient jugé opportun et nécessaire de revendiquer une forme de constitutionalisation des droits économiques et sociaux, se fondant a priori sur le statut de droit de ces droits.

La dynamique de la Charte canadienne

Au-delà des débats engendrés par les fonctions juridiques et politiques spécifiques de la *Charte canadienne des droits et libertés*, ce sont les articles 7, 15 et 1 de la Charte qui ont soulevé certains espoirs relatifs à la sauvegarde de *l'espace social*[10] canadien. Cependant, tout porte à croire que la compétence de la Charte en matière de droits économiques et sociaux tend à être de plus en plus niée lorsqu'elle ne laisse pas les citoyens devant une ambiguïté des plus hermétique.

On connaît l'énigme que représente, aux fins de la reconnais-sance des droits sociaux et économiques, la conjugaison des exigences de la Cour suprême en matière de discrimination. Les expressions *caractéristiques personnelles* et *minorité discrète et isolée*[11] font couler beaucoup d'encre; il s'agit de savoir si certaines dimensions de la condition sociale des personnes pauvres sont assimilables, par analogie, aux caractéristiques personnelles qui isolent les individus les plus démunis et comportent ainsi des effets discriminatoires.[12] Dans le meilleur des mondes cependant, il est clair que l'article 15 de la Charte n'a pas pour objet de corriger l'effet des politiques économiques qui portent atteinte aux droits de catégories de citoyens. Récemment, dans une affaire d'assurance-chômage où il était question de l'assurabilité d'emplois non liés aux affaires principales de l'employeur, la Cour d'appel fédérale concluait assez hâtivement que les *caractéristiques de l'emploi n'étaient pas celles de l'employé* et que ce genre de situation ne saurait être visée par l'article 15 de la Charte.[13]

N'est-il pas aussi significatif que nous nous demandions encore si certaines *dimensions économiques* de *certains droits* ne pourraient pas mettre en péril la sécurité de la personne au sens de l'article 7 de cette derniere?[14]

Par ailleurs, toute tentative d'inclure la protection de certaines dimensions des droits économiques et sociaux dans la Charte sera soumise aux contours incertains des limitations aux droits que permet l'article 1 de la Charte. En effet, depuis la décision de la Cour suprème dans l'affaire *McKinney*,[15] il est permis d'affirmer non seulement que le test élaboré par M. le juge Dickson dans la décision *Oakes* est révolu mais en sus, qu'en matière de droit social et de législations sociales, l'efficience de l'article 1 de la Charte à titre de verrou de sécurité des droits est bien aléatoire, surtout quand le gouvernement invoquera des motifs s'apparentant à l'argument des limitations plus spécifiquement liées à l'équilibre d'ensemble des programmes sociaux.[16]

Devant une telle logique d'enfermement et d'individualisation du rapport du citoyen à l'état, tout porte à croire qu'il y a lieu de revendiquer un régime constitutionnel spécifique à l'énonciation, à la protection et à la reconnaissance des droits économiques et sociaux. Mais qu'en est-il du débat existant?

Le piège de l'actualisation du fédéralisme canadien

Il paraît inutile de s'étendre ici sur les attaques visant la précarisation de l'ensemble des programmes sociaux au Canada. Il suffit de rappeler que la récente configuration politique, juridique et jurisprudentielle[17] a facilité la mobilisation et la réflexion autour d'un thème commun: le sort des droits sociaux et économiques.

Tout lecteur quelque peu attentif du Rapport Beaudoin-Dobbie[18] et des principaux documents de réflexion relatifs à une "Charte sociale"[19] constate l'évacuation du discours des droits de cette démarche. Attitude défensive s'il en est une, il s'agit dans tous les cas d'éloigner autant que faire se peut le justiciable de la justiciabilité en l'espèce. On remarquera les expressions choisies par le Comité Beaudoin-Dobbie, lesquelles réfèrent exclusivement aux *objectifs sociaux*[20] d'un Canada renouvelé et aux *engagements sociaux* de l'État.[21] Pour le Comité, la Charte confère des *droits* aux citoyens et les articles 7 et 15 de la Charte ne peuvent exprimer les *engagements* que les gouvernements doivent prendre envers l'ensemble de la société.[22] Devant cette différence de *nature* entre les droits civils et politiques et les *objectifs* sociaux, le Comité propose que les gouvernements s'engagent à favoriser l'atteinte des objectifs sociaux[23] en vertu de l'enchâssement de principes *générateurs de responsabilités.*[24] La concrétisation de ces objectifs sociaux doit continuer de relever du gouvernement.[25]

Il s'avère que ces principes générateurs de responsabilités[26] relèvent d'abord du souci d'assurer le pouvoir de dépenser du gouvernement central et non de la reconnaissance des droits des citoyens. Plus étonnant encore, les objectifs sociaux décrits dans la proposition Beaudoin-Dobbie sont loin de constituer une liste adéquate des droits économiques et sociaux dont on pourrait revendiquer l'enchâssement constitutionnel, sans compter que certains postulent l'existence de valeurs communes à la pertinence douteuse. Ainsi qu'en est-il du droit des travailleurs à la syndicalisation et à la négociation, dépouillé de l'affirmation du droit de grève; et du droit à des prestations sociales adéquates, dépourvues d'une qualification essentielle, à savoir qu'elles doivent viser à garantir un niveau de vie décent. Qu'en est-il de la dimension positive du droit au travail, laquelle s'exprime essentiellement par le droit à une politique de l'emploi effective? Seul le respect de l'environnement fait figure de nouvel acquis dans les modifications proposées à la *Loi constitutionnelle de 1982* par l'ajout d'un éventuel article 36.1. Somme toute, les recommandations du Rapport Beaudoin-Dobbie n'ont strictement rien a voir avec les droits économiques et sociaux. Elles concernent plutôt le financement des politiques sociales au sein d'un Canada renouvelé. Nous ne prétendons pas qu'il soit inutile de sécuriser de la sorte ces engagements au sein de la fédération canadienne, loin de là. Nous affirmons seulement que le Pacte social est un piège interprétatif et réductionniste de la portée et de la nature des droits économiques et sociaux. Peu importe la somme de législations sociales que l'on tente de sauvegarder si le processus constitutionnel éloigne les citoyens de la possibilité de retourner le gouvernement à sa table de travail lorsque les lois ou les politiques sociales ne sont pas conformes à l'ensemble des droits de la personne. Pour ce faire, nous croyons qu'il faut poser la question de la constitutionalisation des droits et de la justiciabilité de ces derniers. Mais au fait, s'agit-il de la même question?

Les droits sociaux: lesquels et comment?

Lors d'une récente communication,[27] le professeur Scott a soumis une présentation schématique de trois conceptualisations possibles en matière de constitutionalisation de droits économiques et sociaux. Le professeur Scott propose d'abord une approche fondée sur l'énonciation de principes directeurs gouvernant l'action étatique. C'est à peu de chose près l'essentiel de la recommandation Beaudoin-Dobbie que nous avons déjà commentée sans toutefois souligner que la recommandation propose aussi de soumettre le contrôle du respect de ces principes directeurs à un processus d'audience publique. La deuxième approche se fonde sur le rôle interprétatif de l'énonciation des droits sociaux et économiques. Malgré certaines ouvertures faites par la Cour suprème en la matière,[28] il nous apparaît que les dernières mouvances relatives à l'article 1 de la Charte[29] annoncent un avenir précaire à une telle proposition; il convient cependant d'en souligner le mérite dans le mesure où les engagements sociaux sont tout au moins énoncés sous forme de droits. Ne s'agit-il pas par ailleurs du sort réservé aux droits économiques et sociaux dans plusieurs pays où la Constitution procéde à une telle énonciation?[30]

Finalement, le professeur Scott, s'inspirant peut-être d'une certaine doctrine essentialiste,[31] propose qu'un noyau dur et incontournable de droits soit directement soumis au contrôle constitutionnel. Cette proposition est certes un concept juridique plus porteur que celui retenu par le législateur québécois qui, bien qu'énonçant certains droits sociaux et économiques dans la *Charte des droits et libertés de la personne*,[32] les vide substantiellement de leur contenu en en restreignant la portée aux mesures prévues par la loi.[33]

C'est à ce stade-ci de l'énoncé des conceptualisations possibles de la constitutionalisation des droits économiques et sociaux que se heurtent les multiples attentes générées par l'application des règles d'interdépendance de l'ensemble des droits entre eux. Le principe de l'interdépendance permet non seulement d'affirmer que l'énonciation des droits sociaux et économiques est insuffisante (même dans les cas où la fonction interprétative d'une telle énonciation offrirait des gages d'effectivité) mais aussi que le respect des engagements internationaux du Canada en matière de droits de la personne et plus spécifiquement des droits économiques et sociaux nécessite aussi une énonciation effective de ces droits dans le respect du principe d'égalité et d'accès à la justice. L'effectivité pose le problème de la justiciabilité alors que celui de l'accès à la justice oblige a garantir aux citoyens et aux groupes d'intérêt communautaires le locus standi nécessaire en regard de droits qui comportent très souvent des as-pects collectifs auxquels nos tribunaux sont peu rompus ou refusent de se rompre. Les aménagements nécessaires en vue du respect de ces principes découlant de droits dépendent cependant du système juridique en cause et du rapport de force opposant les revendicateurs de droits au pouvoir politique.

Ce constat théorique, destiné essentiellement à démontrer que la juridicité des droits économiques et sociaux doit aussi viser à rapprocher la justiciabilité de ces droits du justiciable, nous amène forcément à énoncer quelques réflexions issues de l'hypothese de la saisine par le judiciaire des droits économiques et sociaux, laquelle n'est pas si éloignée de la question de la nature et des limites des droits constitutionnellement enchéssés.

La théorie du noyau dur des droits proposée par le professeur Scott comporte forcément un aspect minimaliste et essentialiste. Cela suffit-il? Pour répondre à cette première question, il faut s'attarder à une deuxième question. Dans un régime juridique dépourvu de tri-bunal constitutionnel oû plusieurs instances[34] sont susceptibles d'être saisies de questions mettant en cause les droits économiques et sociaux enchéssés, est-il raisonnable que les droits économiques et sociaux soient soumis à l'examen du judiciaire? Ces droits étant en constante évolution, il y aurait risque, selon certains, d'éclatement et d'inconsistance dans une jurisprudence issue de diverses provinces et paliers de tribunaux qui pourraient avoir des conceptions différentes de droits tels le droit à l'environnement ou au logement. Par ailleurs, il est d'usage d'affirmer que les législations sociales sont si com-plexes et liées en elles, qu'il est inconcevable de confier aux tribunaux de droit commun la tâche incidente d'élaborer la politique sociale au

Canada. Il est cependant peut-être plus juste de parler d'un certain alourdissement du mandat du judiciaire que d'une appropriation illégitime, dans la mesure ou le Parlement conserverait toujours le pouvoir d'ajuster les législations en vue de les rendre conformes à la Charte sociale suite à l'examen de conformité aux droits sociaux de ces législations.

Ainsi, cet éclatement jurisprudentiel ne constituerait pas une telle menace s'il s'agit uniquement du contrôle du respect d'un noyau dur de droits économiques et sociaux incontournables. D'où l'intérêt de la thèse de l'énonciation constitutionnelle de droits économiques et sociaux justiciables, qui vue ainsi, ne nous éloigne pas tant des aspirations entretenues à l'égard de l'article 7 de l'actuelle Charte des droits et libertés énonçant le droit à la sécurité de sa personne à sous réserve que les garanties constitutionnelles ne soient évidemment pas soumises au fardeau préalable de démontrer une entorse aux principes de justice fondamentale.

Mais y a-t-il des les limites souhaitables à la saisine de ces droits par le judiciaire? Bien sûr, la thèse de la déclaration d'inconstitutionnalité pure et simple n'est pas des plus séduisante. Mais encore ici, n'oublions pas que nous parlons de stratégie défensive, de stratégie de survie. Par ailleurs, la fonction de paix sociale[35] des législations économiques destinées aux travailleurs les moins bien nantis forcera toujours les gouvernements à refaire leurs devoirs. Revendiquer l'invalidation pure et simple n'est donc pas un mince objectif lorsqu'il s'agit de l'invalidation de mesures régressives dont le remplacement suppose l'exercice démocratique parlementaire. Bien sûr, les bénéficiaires des droits sociaux et économiques sont souvent les moins habilités à se faire entendre auprès des instances parlementaires. Cependant, tout porte à croire que la collectivisation accrue des intérêts de ces derniers et la récente visibilité issue des débats entourant la Charte sociale pourraient changer les choses en l'espèce. Ainsi, peu importe l'issue de l'affaire *Schachter*, la seule possibilité de faire déclarer inconstitutionnelle une loi qui ne respecterait pas les droits économiques constitutionnellement garantis constitue une perspective intéressante répondant à une logique minimaliste qui échappe au pièges de l'abrogation pure et simple de dispositions législatives en d'autres matières, tel dans le cas du droit à l'égalité. La thèse essentialiste du professeur Scott suffit donc à supporter la saisine élargie des tribunaux de droit commun en matière de droits sociaux et économiques.

Mais une tendance semble se dessiner au sein des groupes communautaires canadiens à l'effet de créer un Tribunal social dont la juridiction comporterait des pouvoirs d'ordonnance divers et élargis.[37] Nous ne sommes par certaine que cette approche soit souhaitable. D'emblée, nous constatons que ce Tribunal, bien que légitimé par sa composition, ressemble plus à un organe de contrôle de type international qu'à une cour de justice. D'aucuns croient opportun de défendre la souveraineté parlementaire en soumettant explicitement les ordonnances de ce tribunal à la possibilité des parlements de les désavouer dans un délai imparti. Considérant que cela peut tout autant survenir dans le cas des tribunaux de droit commun, bien qu'implicitement nous comprenons mal qu'il soit souhaitable de créer un Tribunal de deuxième zone dont la constitution organique ferait état de ses faiblesses, rendant ainsi la comparaison avec les "vrais" tribunaux d'autant plus odieuse. Nous préférons croire que des droits sont des droits et qu'il est inacceptable que les tribunaux de droit commun ne soient pas contraints à un examen de la législation qui tienne compte de l'ensemble des impératifs juridiques des droits de la personne. Par ailleurs, le mythe de l'expertise requise aux fins de siéger à un tel Tribunal pourrait mal servir les communautés en recul. L'approche essentialiste des droits nécessite-t-elle vraiment une telle d'expertise? En somme, il ne faudrait pas segmenter la justiciabilité des droits de la personne comme on l'a trop longtemps fait de la juridicité de ces derniers.

En conclusion, si la constitutionalisation des droits économiques n'est pas la seule façon de garantir le partage de l'enrichissement collectif et l'accès à la démocratie participative, il s'avère qu'en période de crise sociale, la constitutionalisation de ces droits est un outil nécessaire. Par ailleurs, le droit international dont devraient s'inspirer les tribunaux canadiens s'emploie à élaborer des contenus spécifiques pour des droits dont on admet le flou dans l'énonciation initiale. Il n'y a pas vraiment de raisons juridiques pour que ce raffinement du droit international envers le processus de définition des droits économiques et sociaux n'alimente pas les tribunaux de droit commun ainsi que les tribunaux administratifs, souvent plus accessibles aux citoyens et dorénavant habilités, dans certaines circonstances, à disposer des questions relatives à la Charte.

Notes

1   Voir *N.U. Doc. off.*, *E/1992 (1951)*, pp. 21 et suivantes.

2   Voir l'article 26 du *Pacte international relatif aux droits civils et politiques*. Le Comité des droits de l'homme a eu l'occasion d'éclaircir la portée de cet article et de préciser qu'il concerne l'ensemble des lois adoptées par un état, peu importe qu'elles le soient ou non en application des droits et engagements énoncés audit Pacte. Voir l'affaire *Zwaan-de-vries* c. *Pays-Bas*, communication no.182/1984 et *L.G. Danning* c. *Pays-Bas*, communication no.180/1984.

3   Voir entre autres *Indivisibilite et interdépendance des droits économiques, sociaux, culturels, civils et politiques*, A.G. Rés. 41/114 (1986); A.G. Rés. 42/102 et 42/49 (1987); A.G. Rés. 43/113 et 43/49 (1988); A.G. Rés. 44/130 (1989).

4   Le terme *juridicisation* ou celui de *juridification* réfère à l'existence d'un processus qui fait l'objet de modes de création ou d'application de règles, en l'occurrence de règles normatives juridiques. Voir A.J. Arnaud, *Dictionnaire encyclopédique de théorie et de sociologie du droit*, 1988, p.203.

5   Le terme *justiciabilité* réfère ici à la capacité juridique d'individus ou de collectivités de saisir le judiciaire de questions de droit. L'acception de ce terme est donc beaucoup plus large que la seule question des limites juridictionnelles du tribunal, lorsqu'il sera saisi d'un litige émanant d'une question de droit social.

6   Créé en vertu de la résolution du Conseil économique et social 1985/17, C.E.S. *Doc. off 1985*, Supp. no.1, p.15, E/1985/85.

7   Voir à cet effet, Craig Scott, «The Interdependence and Permeability of Human Rights Norms: Towards a Partial Fusion of the International Covenants on Human Rights» (1989) 27:4Osgoode Hall L.J., p.769.

8   P. Alston, «Conjuring up New Human Rights: A Proposal for Quality Control» (1984) 78 A.J.I.L. 607.

9   Voir sur cette question M. Mandel, *The Charter of Rights and the Legalization of Politics in Canada*, 1989 (Toronto: Wall & Thompson, 1989) et H. Glasbeek, From «Constitutional Rights to 'Real' Rights- "R-I-I-G-HTS FO-OR-WA-ARD HO"!?» (1990) 10 Recueil annuel de Windsor d'accès à la justice 468.

10 Nous empruntons cette expression au droit communautaire européen qui tend à opposer l'espace social à l'espace économique.

11 Expressions tirées des décisions de la Cour suprème dans *Andrews*, [1989] 1 R.C.S. 143 et *Turpin* , [1989] 1 R.C.S. 1332.

12 Notons cependant que, dans une décision du 15 juin 1990, la Cour suprème de la Colombie britannique, disposant d'une requéte en irrecevabilité, statuait que *"...applying the test under s.15 of the Charter, it is clear that persons receiving income assistance constitute a discrete and insular minority*

within the meaning of s. 15. It may be reasonably inferred that because recipients of public assistance generally lack substantial political influence, they comprise those groups in society to whose needs and wishes elected officials have no apparent interest in attending." Federated Anti-Poverty Groups of British Columbia et al c. *Procureur général de la Colombie britannique et al*, No. A893060, jugement de M. le juge Parrett du 15 juin 1990, à la p. 29 et 30.

13 *Procureur général du Canada c. David George*, [1991] 1 C.F. 344 (C.A.F.).

14 Ce questionnement issu de la décision de la Cour suprème dans *Procureur général du Québec* c. *Irwin Toys*, [1989] 1 R.C.S 927 a soulevé des espoirs en matière de droits économiques, lesquels ont cependant été refroidis par les plus récents propos de M. le juge en chef Lamer dans l'affaire du *Renvoi relatif au Code criminel (Man)*, [1990] 1 R.C.S. 1123, 1168 qui appuyait alors les affirmations du juge McIntyre dans l'affaire du *Renvoi relatif à la Public Service Employee Act*, [1987] 1 R.C.S. 313 à l'effet que la Charte ne protége pas les droits sociaux et économiques. Il conviendra de consulter l'excellente étude de la professeure Martha Jackman sur cette question en vue d'une analyse politique, juridique et comparée. Voir Martha Jackman, «The Protection of Welfare Rights Under the Charter» (1988) 20 Revue de droit d'Ottawa, 257.

15 *McKinney c. Université de Guelph*, [1989] 3 R.C.S. 229.

16 Voir sur cette question l'étude complète à laquelle s'est livrée la professeure France Morrissette, «Le droit a l'égalité de la Charte appliqué à certains programmes sociaux fédéraux» (1991) 22 Revue générale de droit, 509.

17 Notons entre autres la récente décision de la Cour suprème du Canada relative aux ententes conclues en vertu du Régime d'assistance publique du Canada dont la pérennité dépend entièrement du Parlement fédéral selon la Cour, *Renvoi relatif au Régime d'assistance publique du Canada*, [1991] 2 R.C.S. 525; les conséquences de la *Loi sur les arrangements fiscaux entre le gouvernement fédéral et les provinces et sur les contributions fédérales en matière d'enseignement postsecondaire et de santé*, L.R.C., C. F-8 (telle qu'amendée par S.C. 1986, c.34) ainsi que de la nouvelle *Loi canadienne sur la santé*, S.C. 1984, c.6. De plus, les propositions fédérales de septembre 1991 relatives à l'union économique canadienne (*Shared Values*) évacuaient complètement toute reconnaissance de la pauvreté et de ses conséquences ainsi que l'existence même des droits sociaux et économiques aux fins du respect des engagements qui en découlent.

18 Rapport du comité mixte spécial sur le renouvellement du Canada, 28 février 1992.

19 Dont le document de travail ontarien intitulé *"Une charte sociale canadienne, la consolidation de nos valeurs communes"*, Ministère des affaires intergouvernementales, septembre 1991.

20 Cette façon de s'engager à réaliser l'atteinte d'objectifs sociaux plutôt que de droits rappelle les récents et moins récents débats européens relatifs à l'élaboration de la *Charte sociale européenne* (S.T.E. no. 35, 1961) et de la

Charte communautaire des droits sociaux fondamentaux des travailleurs adoptée par le Conseil des ministres de la C.E.E. en décembre 1989. Dans les deux cas cependant, il est clair que l'on s'est aussi appliqué à déjuridiciser le social au profit d'une vision économique des engagements sociaux des états. Voir dans le plus récent cas de la Déclaration adoptant la *Charte sociale communautaire*, éliane Vogel Polsky, «Quel futur pour l'Europe sociale après le sommet de Strasbourg?» (1990) 2 Droit social, p. 219.

[21] Voir Rapport du Comité, p.85.

[22] Laquelle semble ici vivre en parfaite dissociation avec les citoyens eux-mêmes.

[23] Lesquels ne sont toujours pas l'expression d'engagements découlant de la reconnaissance de droits.

[24] On comprend bien que c'est avant tout la fédération qui génère de telles responsabilités et non les droits des citoyens et collectivités. Ces responsabilités seront par ailleurs soumises au seul contrôle de l'électorat. Cette dernière proposition contribue pleinement à entretenir le mythe de la démocratie participative, mythe particulièrement odieux à l'endroit des groupes de la société victimes de la négation de leurs droits sociaux et économiques.

[25] On constate une fois de plus, une déroutante confusion entre le caractère de *droit* des droits économiques et sociaux et les limites potentielles de la justiciabilité de ces derniers. Cette confusion est certes politiquement plus rentable que la bête admission à l'effet que l'état n'entend accorder aucune forme de reconnaissance à des droits dont la nature juridique ne fait aucun doute.

[26] Les gouvernements seraient tenus de favoriser l'atteinte de l'intégralité, de l'universalité, de la transférabilité, de la gestion publique et de l'accessibilité des soins de santé seulement; l'atteinte de services sociaux et des prestations sociales adéquates, une éducation de qualité, certains droits des travailleurs et le respect de l'environnement. Voir Rapport du Comité, p.85.

[27] Voir Craig Scott "Social Values Projected and Protected in a Renewed Canadian Constitution: A Brief Appraisal of the Federal and Ontario Government Proposals" dans *Constitutional Commentaries: An Assessment of The Federal Constitutional Proposals*, (Kingston: Institute of Intergovernmental Relations, 1992), D. Brown, R. Young et D. Herperger, Éds.

[28] Voir *Slaight Communications c. Davidson*, [1989] 1 R.C.S. 1038.

[29] Voir *supra*, note 16.

[30] Pour une étude de cette question à l'échelle de la Communauté européenne, consultez Brian Bercusson, «Fundamental Social and Economic Rights in the European Community» dans *Droits de l'homme et communauté européenne: vers 1992 et au-delà*, European University Institute, Florence,

1989; Lothar Zechklin, *Les droits fondamentaux dans la jurisprudence du Tribunal constitutionnel fédéral de la R.F.A.*, [1990] 31 C. de D. 641; Collectif droit public positif, *Cours constitutionnelles européennes et droits fondamentaux*, Actes du Colloque d'Aix-en Provence, février 1981.

[31] Voir J.W. Nickel, *Making Sense of Human Rights*, (Berkeley: U. of California Press, 1987) et J.W.Nickel et R. Martin, «Recent Work on the Concept of Rights» 17:3 (juillet 1980) American Philosophical Quarterly, 165.

[32] *Charte des droits et libertés de la personne*, L.R.Q., c. C-12, articles 39 et suivants, lesquels soumettent systèmatiquement les "droits-créances" aux limites prescrites par la loi, les vidant ainsi, de leur contenu substantif.

[33] Voir à titre d'exemples, les récentes décisions: *Lévesque* c. *Procureur général du Québec*, [1988] R.J.Q. 223 (le fait d'être étudiant ne saurait constituer une situation s'apparantant à la condition sociale aux fins de l'éligibilité à l'aide sociale, laquelle exclut par voie réglementaire l'éligibilité des étudiants à l'aide); *Lecours* c. *Procureur général du Québec* J.E. 90-638 (C.S.) (en appel) (la Charte québécoise n'accorde pas un droit universel à l'aide sociale mais garantit simplement le droit prévu par la Loi); *Méthot* c. *Commission des affaires sociales du Québec*, J.E. 91-1120 (C.S.) (Id.); *Robitaille-Rousseau* c. *Commission scolaire Montcalm* J.E. 911-378 (C.S.) (le droit à l'instruction publique gratuite est garanti dans la mesure prévue par la Loi). Notons d'une part que les droits sociaux et économiques garantis par la Charte des droits et libertés de la personne ne sont pas des droits "protégés" au sens de l'article 52 de la Charte qui édicte qu'aucune disposition législative d'une loi du Québec, même postérieure à la Charte, ne saurait déroger à cette dernière. Cependant, le droit à la séreté et à l'intégrité de sa personne énoncé à l'article 1 de la Charte fait partie desdites dispositions protégées, bien que soumises à la clause limitative de l'article 9.1.

[34] Et même certains tribunaux administratifs compte tenu des récents développements de la Cour suprème en la matière.

[35] Robert D. Bureau, Katherine Lippel et Lucie Lamarche, «Développement et tendances du droit social au Canada, (1940-1984)» dans *Le droit de la famille et le droit social au Canada*, volume 49 des études commandées dans le cadre de la Commission royale sur l'union économique et les perspectives de développement du Canada, I. Bernier et A. Lajoie Éds., Approvisionnements et Services Canada, 1986,pp. 79 – 147.

[36] Voir Mars 1992, Communiqué de presse, "Alternative Social Charter Proposed by Groups across Canada," et Appendice I.

4

Social Charter Issues

Gwen Brodsky*

Introduction

The *Charter of Rights* has produced few gains for poor Canadians. In its early years, many people hoped that governments would see the *Charter*, especially the equality guarantee, as requiring legislative action to address the persistent and pervasive inequality of certain groups in Canadian society. Instead, with few exceptions, governments have vigorously resisted any suggestion that the *Charter* requires positive action. In litigation, government lawyers have taken the position that ss. 7 and 15 are nothing but guarantees of formal equality and procedural fairness. Too often this formalistic, liberal point of view on the *Charter* has held sway, with the result that some people are attracted to the possibility of a new and better social charter that directs governments to take positive steps to address problems such as poverty, homelessness, and violence against women and children. These are problems that can only be addressed by government action, the antithesis of the government restraint required by liberal constitutional theory.

The social charter was a prominent theme in all five of the national constitutional conferences sponsored by the federal government during January and February of 1992. A clear consensus emerged at both the Montreal conference of February 1-2 and at the final conference in Vancouver on February 15-16 that a social charter must be discussed. At some point during the conference process, Constitutional Affairs Minister Joe Clark, who initially opposed the idea, softened his stand against entrenchment of a social charter, and by February was inviting its proponents to come up with details. Efforts to achieve official recognition for the idea of a social charter crystallized on March 2, 1992 with the release of the Beaudoin-Dobbie *Report*. The Beaudoin-Dobbie Committee recommended that the Constitution be amended to include a clause called a "social covenant." The clause was adopted by a majority of provincial premiers at the multilateral constitutional negotiations in the Spring and Summer of 1992, and is the basis of the "social union" clause in the Charlottetown Accord.[1]

Do We Want a Social Charter?

During the winter of 1991-92, the Beaudoin-Dobbie Committee heard diverse and sometimes conflicting submissions concerning the idea of a social charter. Support for the idea was very strong. To work out the details, such as whether a social charter should be enforced by the courts, public discussion was needed. That discussion was never allowed to take place. It is unfortunate that the Beaudoin-Dobbie Committee did not endorse the idea of a national conference on the social charter, rather than proposing the social covenant that it did. The Beaudoin-Dobbie social covenant proposal, which was substantially reproduced in the Charlottetown Accord, is not a strong commitment. Its coverage is inadequate. It contains no effective enforcement mechanism. It does not even clearly establish a forum for hearings concerning allegations that governments have breached the covenant, although public hearings of some kind are contemplated. Also, it has conflicting values built right into it. On the one hand, it purports to bind governments to social commitments such as health care. On the other hand, it endorses market-place values such as the four freedoms, which may conflict with those social commitments. It is revealing that in the Premiers' Unity Proposal, and the Charlottetown Accord that followed, this mixed bag of competing values is called a "Social and Economic Union" clause. Overall, these proposed clauses certainly do not fare well when measured against the standard of Canada's commitments in international human rights agreements.

The proposals do not commit governments to the development of any new social programs. Ironically, the Beaudoin-Dobbie social covenant and the Charlottetown Accord's social and economic union clauses do not even purport to entrench existing social programs. This comes as something of a surprise to anyone aware of the history of these clauses and familiar with Ontario's social charter proposal, which was released on February 13, 1992. The central objective of that proposal was to prevent the federal government from withdrawing from cost-sharing agreements in the way that it backed out of its commitment to Ontario, Alberta and British Columbia under the Canada Assistance Plan in 1990. In a similar vein, the British Columbia Committee on the Constitution decided that "the main impetus to having a social charter is to prevent the disintegration of existing social programs," and on April 2, 1992 came forward with a proposal for a social covenant that would do nothing but entrench existing cost-sharing agreements.[2] The Charlottetown Accord falls considerably short of entrenching existing cost-sharing arrangements. Instead, it protects, for only a maximum of five years, such agreements from unilateral change.

The trouble with the Charlottetown Accord's social union recommendation is not only that it is modest in what it attempts to do. The social union is part of a package of political compromises that includes a mechanism for increased devolution of federal spending powers, and a companion provision for the free movement of persons, services and capital, the beginnings of a common market, and a Canada clause that may weaken existing constitutional protections for members of disadvantaged groups. Furthermore, if the Charlottetown Accord's social union clause is entrenched, it may be viewed by judges as a justification for restricting the application of ss. 7 and 15 of the *Charter of Rights* to circumstances that do not seem to involve questions about social and economic policy; in other words, it may be used as a jurisdictional reason for declining to grant remedies in cases involving the claims of poor people. In my opinion, we are better off with no social charter than with the Charlottetown Accord's social union. The difficulty is that there is so much momentum behind the idea of some kind of social and economic rights protection that it is now firmly a part of the constitutional agenda.

However, let us assume that adoption of the Charlottetown Accord's social union is not inevitable, and that it is still possible to secure a different kind of social and economic rights protection. In other words, let us suppose we are just beginning to have the discussion that people might have wanted to have at a national conference on the idea of a social charter. In that case, there are a number of issues to consider. A social charter could be either good or bad, depending on various contingencies. Canadian governments are suffering from a lack of will to take the necessary measures to redress the persistent inequality of historically disadvantaged groups in our society, to end poverty and homelessness, and to halt the systematic degradation of the environment. Our governments are not living up to the commitments that Canada has made in international human rights agreements. To provide but one example, by ratifying the 1966 International Covenant on Economic, Social and Cultural Rights, Canada recognized the right of everyone to an adequate standard of living, including the right to housing, and agreed to undertake all necessary measures for the realization of that right. And yet, British Columbia families with children remain virtually defenceless against discrimination in housing, notwithstanding a long history of demands from the public and the New Democratic Party for amendments to the *British Columbia Human Rights Act* to provide protections for children and their families.[3]

To be sure, concerns about preserving existing social programs are also legitimate. Social programs are already threatened by the Canada-U.S. Free Trade Agreement, and by the desire of the federal government to reduce its obligations for cost-sharing. Social programs stand to be further eroded by the downward harmonization that could result from interprovincial competition encouraged by economic union and a common market. A social charter that protected existing social programs and promoted additional legislative measures, such as employment equity and increases in minimum wage levels necessary for the fulfillment of social and economic rights commitments, would be a good thing, without question. But a social charter, which sounds good but has the effect of undermining existing social programs, discouraging the creation of new social programs, or weakening existing constitutional protections for members of disadvantaged groups, would be a bad thing. What then are the contingencies that determine what the effects of a social charter would be? The first is the question of trade-off. From the perspective of economically and socially disadvantaged groups, defeating the proposals for economic union and diminished federal spending powers must be seen as a non negotiable priority of provincial governments. A social charter gained at the expense of abandoning opposition to such proposals would not be worth the cost. The net effect of the exchange would be a loss for disadvantaged groups in Canada. This conclusion is virtually irresistible when one considers the inadequacies of the Charlottetown Accord or even the Ontario government's proposals, but it is difficult to conceive of any social charter that would be an effective counterweight to the federal government's agenda to achieve free movement of persons, services and capital and to decrease its responsibility for social programs. Assuming that the required level of support for a social charter could be obtained without such trade-offs, having a social charter could be a good thing, depending on various contingencies concerning its content and relationship to existing constitutional rights.

What Kind of Social Charter?

Turning first to the question of content, the fact is that, right from the beginning, different people have been envisioning different things when they have talked about a social charter. In particular, some people have imagined a social charter that entrenches certain fundamental entitlements, establishing them as justiciable constitutional rights. Others have imagined various kinds of non-justiciable mechanisms. A justiciable right is a right that can be enforced by the courts. A justiciable constitutional right is one which gives the courts ultimate power over governments, subject to the power of governments to invoke an override provision such as that contained in s. 33 of the *Charter*. In the fall of 1991, the position of the National Anti-Poverty Organization (NAPO) was that new justiciable social and economic rights should be entrenched in the Constitution to the effect that:

1) Everyone has the right to an adequate standard of living, including adequate food, clothing and housing.

2) Everyone has the right to work, which includes the right of everyone to the opportunity to gain his or her living by work which he or she freely chooses or accepts.

3) Everyone has the right to the enjoyment of just and favourable conditions of work which ensure, in particular:

   a) Remuneration which provides all workers, at a minimum, with:

      i) Fair wages and equal remuneration for work of equal value without distinction of any kind;

      ii) A decent living for themselves and their families;

   b) Safe and healthy working conditions;

   c) Equal opportunity for everyone to be promoted in his or her employment to an appropriate higher level, subject to no considerations other than those of seniority and competence;

   d) Rest, leisure and reasonable limitation of working hours and periodic holidays with pay, as well as remuneration for public holidays.

4) Everyone has the right to social security, including social insurance.

5) Everyone has the right to the enjoyment of the highest attainable standard of physical and mental health.

6) Everyone has the right to education.

7) Higher education shall be made equally accessible to all, on the basis of capacity, by every appropriate means.

The premise of proposals such as these, calling for new justiciable social and economic rights, would seem to be that the wording of the existing *Charter of Rights* is deficient. Subsequently, NAPO put its support behind the non-justiciable "Alternative Social Charter."[4] Still, there remains among equality rights and antipoverty activists a concern that neither s. 7 (life, liberty and security of the person and the right not to be deprived thereof except in accordance with principles of fundamental justice) nor s. 15 (equality) will be applied to protect the interests of people who are poor. Indeed, there are court decisions that make such concerns justified. For example, courts have refused to intervene to extend to tenants of public housing procedural protections that tenants of non-subsidized housing are accorded by law, such as the right to adequate notice of eviction. The Nova Scotia courts rejected the *Charter* claims of Ms. Bernard, a single mother dependent on family benefits who was evicted along with her son from Dartmouth public housing without being informed of the reason for her eviction, without being afforded an opportunity to answer in her defence, and upon notice shorter by half than that which the *Residential Tenancies Act* required be given to a tenant of non-subsidized housing. Ms. Bernard's "security of the person" claim was rejected on the basis that security of the person does not apply to economic benefits. Her equality claim was also rejected, on the basis that a person who "freely takes advantage" of benefits provided under a scheme designed for relief of poverty does so with "knowledge of the disadvantages" (*Bernard* (1989))[5]. The disturbing implication of the *Bernard* decision is that *Charter* rights do not apply to a person in receipt of social assistance, such as welfare or public housing.

Fortunately, *Bernard* and other lower court decisions to a similar effect are not the last word on the matter. Whereas some earlier *Charter* decisions of lower courts, including *Bernard*, purported to create a distinction between economic interests and noneconomic interests, recent decisions of the Supreme Court of Canada indicate that the critical distinction is not economic versus non-economic, but rather corporate – commercial economic interests versus the interests of disadvantaged groups; in other words, the important question is not "what is claimed?" but rather "who is claiming?". In *Irwin Toy* (1989),[6] the Supreme Court of Canada held that a corporation is not entitled to claim the protection of "security of the person," and expressly refrained from pronouncing upon whether "economic rights fundamental to human life or survival are to be treated as though they are of the same ilk as corporate-commercial economic rights." The Court reasoned that the inclusion of "security of the person" and the exclusion of "property" from s. 7 leads to an inference that s. 7 does not protect a general "economic liberty" and that a "corporation's economic rights" find no constitutional protection in that section. As for other types of economic claims brought by human beings, as distinct from corporations, the Court said:

> This is not to declare, however, that no right with an economic component can fall within "security of the person". Lower courts have found that the rubric of "economic rights" embraces a broad spectrum of interests, ranging from such rights, included in various international covenants, as rights to social security, equal pay for equal

work, adequate food, clothing and shelter, to traditional
property-contract rights. To exclude all of these at this
early moment in the history of *Charter* interpretation seems
to us to be precipitous.[7]

I turn then to the question of whether the equality rights
guarantee applies to the economic interests of people who are poor.
A plain reading of s. 15 guarantees Canadians the equal benefit and
protection of the law. The words "benefit" and "protection" were
included in the equality guarantee as a result of amendments designed to overcome jurisprudence under the *Bill of Rights* to the effect
that equality rights apply only to penalties and not to benefits such
as those available under unemployment insurance. There are nu-
merous court decisions in which s. 15 has been applied to benefit
schemes. In addition, there is some authority to the effect that being
a recipient of social assistance is a protected ground under s. 15
(*FAPG v. A.G.B.C.* (1991)).[8] In a series of judgments, the Supreme
Court of Canada has ruled that s. 15 is designed to remedy or prevent discrimination against groups suffering social, political and legal
disadvantage in our society (*Andrews* (1989),[9] *Turpin* (1989),[10] *Swain*
(1991)).[11] In the case of *Edmonton Journal* (1989),[12] four members of
the Supreme Court of Canada held in a dissenting judgment that a
s.15 claim brought by *The Edmonton Journal* must be dismissed because s. 15 does not apply to corporations. The majority of the Court
did not consider this issue because it granted the newspaper company relief under another provision of the *Charter*.

An extensive review of ss. 7 and 15 case law is beyond the
scope of this piece, but on the basis of existing jurisprudence it cannot be said that ss. 7 and 15 are too narrowly worded to apply to the
economic concerns of people who are poor. The better view is that
ss. 7 and 15, as worded, make social and economic rights issues
justiciable, provided that the claimant is not a corporation and that
the alleged violation has occurred as a result of a law. My point is
not to promote naive optimism about the promises of *Charter* litigation,[13] but rather to show that poor people are not completely without
Charter rights, even without a social charter. It would be unfortunate
if support for the idea of entrenching new social and economic rights
fueled a perception that the *Charter*, as worded, does not contain any
justiciable social and economic rights. In a similar vein, we must be
concerned about the possibility that a social charter that is in any

way weaker than the *Charter of Rights* will have the effect of draining existing constitutional rights of their substantive content. To address this problem, any social charter that purports to do more than merely entrench cost-sharing agreements should contain a non-derogation clause such as the following:

> Nothing contained in the social charter derogates from the rights of disadvantaged groups contained in the *Canadian Charter of Rights and Freedoms* or limits the ability of anyone whose rights or freedoms, as guaranteed by the *Charter*, have been infringed or denied to apply to a court of competent jurisdiction to obtain a remedy, pursuant to the Charter.[14]

The Charlottetown Accord states that: "A clause should be added to the Constitution stating that the Social and Economic Union does not abrogate or derogate from the Canadian Charter of Rights and Freedoms." The above might provide a model for this.

It is strongly arguable that ss. 7 and 15 require, at minimum:

1. equality in the content and administration of all government benefit schemes, including social assistance,

2. that in no circumstance shall individuals be required to forfeit constitutional rights as a condition of receiving social assistance, and

3. that the grounds and procedures implemented to refuse or terminate benefits designed to meet basic needs must satisfy the requirements of fundamental justice.

Notwithstanding the theoretical potential of ss. 7 and 15 to assist poor people in asserting claims to rights such as these, the reality is that the *Charter* has not produced many gains for poor people during the first ten years of its existence. In my view, however, this reality is not the result of deficient wording, but rather is a reflection of three other factors:

1. governments' unwillingness to undertake progressive law reforms voluntarily,

2. lack of access by poor people to the resources necessary to engage in the litigation process,

3. regressive, anti-egalitarian positions advanced in the courts by governments, and

4. judicial insensitivity to the problems of group disadvantage.

Those are the common problems that all disadvantaged groups in Canada have experienced under the *Charter*. That said, it would be helpful to add an interpretive clause to the *Charter* clarifying that *Charter* rights are to be interpreted in light of substantive commitments Canada has made in international human rights agreements or, better still, in light of commitments that Canada will make in a social charter such as the antipoverty "Draft Social Charter." Such an interpretive clause could be a key component of a social charter. The aim of proposing this clause is not to increase judicial powers, but rather to promote interpretations of the *Charter* that are consistent with the goal of redressing group disadvantage and to overcome, once and for all, the view that social programs should be immune from constitutional review.[15]

'It must be conceded that there is an issue about how far the *Charter* can be pushed to require governments to address the substantive conditions of impoverishment that characterize the lives of members of disadvantaged groups. Although ss. 7 and 15 could be used, and to a very limited extent already have been used, to challenge discrimination and procedural unfairness in social benefit programs, it is unclear whether ss. 7 and 15 will be interpreted to authorize judicial review on the basis of substantive inadequacy. For example, it is not clear that ss. 7 and 15 authorize a judge to enter into an inquiry concerning the adequacy of social assistance rates at the behest of a homeless person. To provide another example, it is quite unlikely that ss. 7 and 15 will be interpreted to permit a court to review a government decision to spend money on a domed stadium rather than on the provision of subsidized housing to people who are homeless. Given this uncertainty, should the wording of the *Charter* be altered to increase the powers of courts to engage in substantive review of government spending decisions, or would it be preferable to create an alternative forum for the adjudication of what might be called pure poverty claims or substantive inadequacy problems? Some people are of the view that any uncertainty regarding the rights of poor people to seek substantive remedies to poverty itself should be resolved by means of a constitutional amendment.

This is what I understand to lie at the heart of the early efforts of NAPO and other antipoverty groups to insert *new* justiciable social and economic rights in the *Charter*. In my view, the idea of establishing new justiciable social and economic rights, by means of constitutional amendment, has problems. Given that poor people, by definition, have fewer resources than anyone else to engage in *Charter* litigation, and given that judicial attitudes favour advantaged groups, what we are likely to experience if such an amendment should become law is an explosion of threatening challenges brought by members of relatively advantaged groups to measures designed to benefit disadvantaged groups.[16]

It is highly unlikely that the enjoyment of new social and economic rights would be limited to poor people. Seven years of *Charter* equality rights litigation shows that courts are more accessible to powerful groups than to disadvantaged groups. Most cases in the sex-equality field consist of challenges brought by men, many of them challenges to laws and programs designed to overcome the inequality of women. Women's rights organizations involved in *Charter* litigation, such as the Legal Education and Action Fund (LEAF), have been forced to devote most of their resources to damage control, i.e., interventions in cases that are threatening to women. Comfort cannot be taken from a counter-argument to the effect that standing to bring social and economic rights challenges could be restricted to members of disadvantaged groups, by means of effective constitutional drafting. Firstly, economic disadvantage is a relative term, not easily reduced to a category that keeps the wrong plaintiffs out but allows the right plaintiffs in. Secondly, members of advantaged groups are quite capable of securing the assistance of members of disadvantaged groups to advance their claims. For example, note to the *Tomen* (1987)[17] litigation in Ontario, in which the Ontario Teachers' Federation (a group of men) is attempting to dismantle the Women Teachers Federation. The men's case is a sex-equality challenge under s. 15. Their plaintiff is a woman.

In my opinion, this is not the time to increase judicial powers by amending the *Charter* to encourage judges to review social programs for their adequacy. The risk of losing what we have is too great. In addition, if they are forced to intervene to defend against threatening challenges, there could be a substantial drain on the very limited resources of the antipoverty groups. The better course for antipoverty activists is to pursue litigation strategies designed to build a body of positive *Charter* jurisprudence and raise public awareness of poverty issues, over a longer period of time. Such a course, while slow, has the virtue of giving antipoverty organizations some measure of control over the content and timing of efforts to use the courts to advance the claims of poor people. To make strategic litigation by antipoverty groups possible, provincial funding must be made available to members of disadvantaged groups. Many of the concerns of poor people fall under provincial rather than federal jurisdiction. Prior to the release of the federal government's 1992 budget, I would have said that the best way for this to be done would be by means of provincial government contributions to the Court Challenges Program. Now that the Court Challenges Program has been cancelled, greater initiative is required from the provincial governments. A co-ordinated federal-provincial program, with one administrative body, would still be the most cost-effective mechanism.

However, the fact that increasing judicial powers may be problematic, does not mean that governments should do nothing in response to public pressure for a social charter. Too often, the social charter has been equated with increased justiciability, with the result that some elected officials may have failed to give serious attention to the idea. If the justiciability issue were set aside, perhaps governments would be able to hear what the real underlying concerns of disadvantaged groups are, and respond to them more imaginatively. Disadvantaged groups need an instrument that guarantees them a voice in political decision making about social and economic policy, an instrument that does not weaken the *Charter* but supplements it and serves as an interpretive aid to the *Charter*. The Charlottetown Accord may make the federal government incapable of creating Canada-wide cost-shared programs such as a national child care scheme, and exacerbate the problem of governments' inability to act independently of market forces. Canada as a whole needs an instrument to prod government implementation of nationwide programs consistent with a healthy environment and the social values, such as women's equality, expressed in the international human rights agreements to which Canada is a signatory.

The Charlottetown Accord's social union does not accomplish what is needed in a social charter. A social charter should contain, at minimum, detailed statements of principles and rights that could be revised and expanded, and should establish an independent monitoring body and determine its powers. A social charter should affirm that everyone has an equal right to well-being, including a right to an adequate standard of living (food, clothing, housing, child care and support services, health care, education, access to employment and just and favourable conditions of work, and the right of workers to organize and bargain collectively). The monitoring body should be given powers and procedures akin to those of a Royal Commission or a provincial ombudsman; for example, the power to request public consultations, research, education, and inquiries. Additional powers should include the power to establish reporting requirements, to recommend concrete measures and time limits for governments to improve their performance in specific areas, and the power to establish processes for governments to achieve intergovernmental agreements necessary to achieve the goals expressed in s. 36 of the *Charter* (i.e., "promoting equal opportunities for the well-being of Canadians" and "providing essential public services of reasonable quality to all Canadians"). In the model that I envision, the decisions of such a monitoring body would be enforceable by the courts only insofar as they established process requirements such as reporting. Resort to the courts could be had if governments failed to respect such process requirements. There could also be a tribunal empowered to hear citizens' complaints of government non-compliance. However, I would not favour a model that gave such a tribunal the power to impose enforceable substantive requirements on governments. Although some people will regard such a model as unsatisfactory because it is ultimately toothless, the advantages of a toothless model, provided it is respected by governments and the public, are several:

1. the power of public embarrassment can be significant – as experience with effective provincial ombudsmen in British Columbia has shown.

2. such a body could have the flexibility to focus on the most serious systemic social and economic problems of our times; in other words, to control its own agenda, as well as the flexibility to be selective in its decisions about who is granted hearings.

3. such a body could be more suited than courts to the adjudication of substantive inadequacy problems, by virtue of its
composition and the resources that could be made available
to it; indeed, the test of such a body's success would be its
capacity to effectively address the very types of problems
that courts do not address well.

4. the disadvantages of a court-centred model of enforcement
are avoided, and

5. the likelihood of government manipulation of appointments,
designed to undermine the body's effectiveness, are reduced.

It is essential that poor people be included in the process of
establishing any new institution that has responsibilities in connection with social and economic rights. Inclusion means, at minimum,
participation in the process of establishing the content of a social
charter, the mandate of the enforcement body and its composition,
and representation within that body.

Governments should now shift their debates about a social
charter to a level of increased sophistication. It is time to rise above
the exchange of platitudes concerning the value that Canadians place
on our social programs, and the virtues of government by politicians
rather than by judges. It is time that governments forged a partner-
ship with the equality rights organizations, antipoverty groups, and
social justice organizations favouring a social charter, and turned
their energies towards the development of a social charter that will
serve Canada well. The Alternative Social Charter discussed in more
detail by Jennifer Nedelsky and Craig Scott in this volume, which
represents the outcome of intense discussions among a large number
of equality rights groups, social justice groups and antipoverty groups
from across Canada, would be a good place to start.

Endnotes

* I wish to acknowledge the intellectual company, criticism and inspiration
that Bruce Porter has generously provided to me, in connection with the
subject of this paper. I am also grateful to Barbara Cameron of NAC, for
her insightful comments. An earlier version of this paper appeared in
Points of View/Points de vue #2 (Edmonton: Centre for Constitutional Studies, 1992).

[1] Please see Appendices III and IV where the relevant Beaudoin-Dobbie and the Charlottetown Accord provisions are reproduced.

[2] Special Committee on Constitutional Matters, *Report: British Columbia and the Canadian Federation*, April 2, 1992 at 17. (This Committee was formerly known as the Members' Committee on the Constitution).

[3] On July 13, 1992 an amendment adding the ground "family status" to the housing provision of the *Human Rights Act* came into force (*Human Rights Amendment Act, 1992* S.B.C. 1992, c.43). Notwithstanding this positive development, there are many other examples of governments failing to fulfill commitments made by Canada under international human rights instruments. Even in the case of British Columbia, an amendment to the *Human Rights Act* is only the first of many measures needed to address problems of access to housing, and even the amendment to the *Human Rights Act* falls short of providing full protection to children and their families. To provide but one example, the protection is limited to rental accomodation, and, therefore, families with children remain defenceless against discrimination in the sale of condominiums.

[4] See Appendix I and J. Nedelsky and C. Scott, "Constitutional Dialogue" (this volume).

[5] *Bernard* v. *Dartmouth Housing Authority* (4 January 1988) Halifax 60129 (N.S.S.C.), aff'd *Re Bernard and Dartmouth Housing Authority* (1989), 53 D.L.R. (4th) 81 (N.S.C.A.). The reasoning in *Bernard* was applied in *Dartmouth Halifax County Regional Housing Authority* v. *Irma Sparks* (13 April 1992) Halifax 75171 (N.S.C.C.).

[6] *Irwin Toy Ltd.* v. *Que. (A.G.)*, [1989] 1 S.C.R. 927.

[7] *Ibid.* at 1003.

[8] *Federated Anti-Poverty Groups of B.C. et. al.* v. *A.G. B.C.* (15 June 1990) Vancouver A893060 (B.C.S.C.).

[9] *Andrews* v. *Law Society of British Columbia*, [1989] 1 S.C.R. 143.

[10] *R.* v. *Turpin*, [1989] 1 S.C.R. 1296.

[11] *Swain* v. *R.*, [1991] 1 S.C.R. 933.

[12] *Edmonton Journal* v. *A.G. Alberta*, [1989] 2 S.C.R. 1326.

[13] See *Ref. re Criminal Code, ss. 193-195.1(7)(c)*, [1990] 4 W.W.R. 481 (S.C.C.), at 521-523, and its problematic application by the Manitoba Court of Appeal in the poverty-disability case of *Fernandes* v. *Director of Social Services (Winnipeg Central)* (10 June 1992) #91-30-00477.

[14] This clause is similar to one of a number of possible amendments proposed by Professor Craig Scott of the University of Toronto, Faculty of Law: see "Social Values Projected and Protected: A Brief Appraisal of the Federal and Ontario Government Proposals" in D. Brown, R. Young and D. Herperger, eds, *Constitutional Commentaries: An Assessment of the 1991*

Federal Proposals (Kingston: Reflections Paper No. 10, Institute for Intergovernmental Relations, Queen's University) 81-92.

[15] See, for example, *Bernard, supra,* note 5.

[16] See Joel Bakan, "What's Wrong with Social Rights?" (this volume).

[17] *Tomen* v. *Ontario Public School Teachers' Federation* (1987), 17 O.A.C. 189 (Div. Ct.); *Re Tomen* (1987), 61 O.R. (2d) 489 (H.C.).

5

Constitutional Dialogue

Jennifer Nedelsky and Craig Scott[*]

Introduction: Texts and Matter

The Alternative Social Charter (ASC) was originally drafted and presented as an alternative to the Ontario government's proposed social
charter. It was endorsed in principle by a wide variety of equality-
seeking social action groups and continues to be relevant as an
example of what an effective and egalitarian social charter might
look like. In particular, it offers a model enforcement mechanism
that we believe should be part of any social charter in the Constitution. At the most general level, the ASC provides a concrete example
of how a rights strategy might be used by those committed to the
gradual, imperfect, and inevitably problematic reshaping of our political structures in the direction of social justice. The ASC extends
formal constitutional recognition of the existence of disadvantaged
groups in Canada and, in giving their voices and claims a formal
priority, tacitly acknowledges that structural injustice creates the mul-
tiple forms of disadvantage that characterize Canadian society. It
extends to the least advantaged a new way of using the language of

rights and the institutional structures of power, which have been so effectively used by the advantaged.

At the least, it could provide a tool for defensive action in the face of claims in the name of "market forces" for erosion of social programs. At its best, the ASC is a bold, imaginative alternative to the dominant American vision of rights as trumps[1] and of the courts as the central means for institutionalizing rights. The ASC makes issues of democratic representation and participation central (rather than oppositional or peripheral) to the meaning of rights. And it presents rights claims in a context conducive to an understanding of rights as vehicles for structuring relations of equality – where the interpretive emphasis can be on patterns of relationships rather than formal, individualistic equality.[2] We argue for the virtues of the ASC with grand visions of its transformative potential and extremely modest expectations about the probable effects of entrenching such a document in the Constitution. Both seem important to us.

Of course we know that many of our colleagues committed to social justice oppose strategies of using legal rights to effect the kinds of fundamental changes we all think are necessary. Since we share so many of their judgements about the limits of legal reform and the deep structural changes necessary to make this society a genuinely just one, it seems appropriate to comment briefly on why we make a different *strategic* judgement about endorsing the ASC and its approach to rights discourse.

First we want to emphasize that we do not simply endorse *any* social charter. For example, we were persuaded that the proposed "Social Covenant" in the Beaudoin-Dobbie *Report* was probably worse than nothing. More broadly, we make no claim that legal rights set in opposition to democratic decision making (which still partly informs the structure of the ASC) is the optimal way to conceptualize or institutionalize the relations of equality to which we aspire. But in opting for the *Charter of Rights and Freedoms*, Canadian society committed itself to making rights a central part of its political discourse. Further, rights discourse represents an increasingly common feature of international politics. In this context, we do not see the wholesale rejection of "rights talk" as a viable political option. The quest then becomes how to use and transform the meanings of rights as well as the institutional mechanisms which continuously shape those meanings in the process of interpreting and enforcing

rights. The project must be to find mechanisms that not only provide protection for those most in need of it, but reshape our
understanding of rights in the process. As we hope to show, the
ASC, or something close to it, could be such a mechanism.

The judgement about the desirability of such a project turns
in part on how one sees the role of legal rights in the deep structures
of injustice in Canada. There is a legitimate fear that a focus on
constitutional rights, and on rights which seem to entrench a "social
services" model of equality, will only serve to divert attention from
the underlying structures (often conceived primarily in economic
terms) that are the real source of inequality.[3] If we were persuaded
that that would be the effect of the ASC, we would oppose it. We
share the objective of political mechanisms that will not simply ameliorate but transform the conditions of inequality. But legal rights *are*
part of the structure of inequality. And the issues that some see as
the real dangers to the disadvantaged – like free trade and corresponding ideologies of competition and market – are themselves
incomprehensible without legal rights of private property and contract. Without imagining that the ASC can transform the political
economy of Canada, we think there is a realistic hope it could contribute (in the long run) to greater democratic control of the meaning
of rights – as well as to the effective participation of those now disadvantaged. We endorse the ASC because we think it holds out the
possibility of institutionalizing rights in ways that will turn political
attention to the underlying structures of inequality that its opponents are concerned about. Whatever its political fate in the short
term, we feel that its arrival on the Canadian political scene will have
implications well into the future for both practical questions of institutional design and theories of rights.

The Alternative Social Charter:
New Forms of Rights

One of the virtues of the ASC is that it facilitates both new understandings and new institutionalizations of rights. In this section we
try to articulate some of the new conceptions of rights that the ASC
would foster and develop. We sketch a vision of rights that we think
is an improvement on dominant images of rights as "trumps,"[4] or
rights as "fences" defining clear boundaries to protected spheres of

liberty.[5] In doing so, we make no claim that ours is the only way to understand rights nor do we present our views here as being much more than schematic. What we do claim, however, is that it matters which way one conceptualizes rights. In particular, we believe that the metaphors we use to describe rights influence the way we understand ourselves and society's arrangements, as well as the potential for changing and deepening those understandings.[6] The way in which rights are phrased carries with it implicit background images about personhood, belonging and the sources of oppression. More narrowly, rights metaphors have strong implications for questions of institutional design, just as the actual or envisaged functioning of institutions can help point the way to more appropriate metaphors for rights. We turn now to the first of our alternative metaphors and its institutional implications.

Rights as sites of dialogue

The metaphor of dialogue

In our view, understanding is deepened if we abandon (or at least limit the all-pervasiveness of) metaphorical language that describes and justifies rights in terms of exclusion and conclusion. That is, we question both the descriptive accuracy and normative value of approaches to rights which emphasize the separateness of persons in society and which point to rights as quasi-absolute, debate-stopping conclusions.[7]

In contrast to the conclusory dimension of the supposed "trumping" quality of rights, we offer the notion of rights as *sites of dialogue*, metaphorical forums in which members of society converse about different claims regarding basic values and relationships. These conversations are governed by the regulative ideal of arriving at mutually acceptable understandings through argument. This metaphor is closely tied to the tradition of rhetoric, according to which legal reasoning (no less than moral or political reasoning, or, for that matter, even scientific reasoning) is best seen as a process of reason giving.[8] Within this enterprise, the underlying purpose is the persuasion of a given audience or interpretive community that an interpretation or application of the law is just, legally correct or meets whatever other criterion for achieving implied or actual assent is meaningful to that audience. Reasoning is about *reasons*, not Reason, about the probable and not the necessary, about the persuasive force of mutually supportive justificatory arguments and not the inexorability of logically entailed conclusions, about the intersubjective validation of claims and not the discovery of some form of external truth.

The metaphor of dialogue offers an understanding of rights which emphasizes their dynamic as opposed to static nature. Rights as rhetoric exist in a "world of ever-shifting shapes and shimmering surfaces".[9] A very similar idea of the dynamic and rhetorical quality of rights has been offered by Martha Minow:

> Legal rights ... should be understood as the language of a continuing process rather than the fixed rules. Rights discourse reaches temporary resting points from which new claims can be made.... Rights in this sense are not 'trumps,' but the language we use to try to persuade others to let us win this round.[10]

We recognize that such accounts can be unsettling, and we cannot in this essay begin to address all the implications, strategic and otherwise, of this choice of metaphor. For the time being, we only draw attention to the words of Ilmar Tammelo, who addresses the instinctive recoiling of many in the face of such rhetorical imagery:

> Where does this process of constant challenge and justification finally come to a rest? In terms of rhetoric the answer is that it never finally does so.... If this seems disquieting it is only because it is forgotten that insights in a changeful human world can only rest assured, and can only remain 'fresh' and viable, through constant challenge and retesting.[11]

Of course this conception of rights as sites of dialogue does not on its own tell us what kinds of substantive arguments and whose voices are involved in the dialogue. Perhaps for this very reason, it may be that the notion of dialogue induces overly naive faith in rights as a source of co-operative dialogue, and obscures and leaves intact entrenched interests and structures. As Minow has put it with respect to the "interpretive turn" in legal scholarship, even as it promises demystification of the law's aura of objectivity, it may replace this with a new mystification, "one that casts an aura of cozy conversation over official acts of domination and control."[12] To the notion of rights as a dialogical claiming process, some kind of notion of rights claiming as an ideological struggle for value space also has to be recognized.[13] To the somewhat idealistic notion of rights as *sites of dialogue* can be added the more realistic notion of rights as *sites of social struggle*, at minimum understood as an interpretive struggle over the ideological meaning of words. Thus, a co-operative regulative ideal could be seen as constantly engaged in a dialectic with some form of a conflict-laden competitive reality.

There are reciprocal implications between conceptions of rights and the institutions that have the authority to define and defend them. If rights are virtual or metaphorical sites of dialogue, it follows (in some nonstringent sense) that such institutions should self-consciously foster actual dialogic processes. There should be overlap and interplay between various institutions and the actors within civil society who invoke their processes. For if rights are sites of dialogue, then so too are rights-interpreting institutions. As we shall argue below, the institutions of the ASC are designed as such sites of dialogue.

Rights institutionalized in this way can overcome (or at least significantly mitigate) their "on-off" quality. As Joel Bakan has argued, with rights you either win or lose; little room is left for ongoing adjustment to new insights and facts or for solutions that represent an integration of both, or many, sides in a legal rights argument.[14] In our view, this is an institutional corollary of the trump metaphor and associated metaphors and, as such, it is not a necessary feature of rights discourse. If rights themselves are seen as metaphorical dialogues, then a corresponding dialogical approach to rights-interpreting institutions suggests an approach within which no one institution has a trumping role (at least in the "medium-term" and certainly not in the long-term). Rights claims become part of, not the end to, political debate. The process of consultation and institutional interplay set in motion by the ASC could thus transform the on-off character of rights as we have come to know them.

The sites of dialogue of the ASC
The first general observation to make is that the ASC is heavily geared toward a multilayered approach that entrenches the interdependence of all constitutional values, as well as interconnections and dialogue

among institutional actors, and between such actors and members of society. There is an emphasis on substantive rights determinations occurring within a relatively fluid, ongoing and never-ending process of mutual persuasion and co-operative scrutiny of shared problems. There is also an emphasis on a multiplicity of forums in which the needs and claims of members of presumptively disadvantaged groups can be heard, acted upon and, in general, taken more seriously by the overall political process.[15] We now take a detailed look at how the institutions of the ASC create those forums.

The Social Rights Council and the Social Rights Tribunal are designed to enhance the extent and quality of social and political dialogue with respect to the rights recognized in s.1 of the ASC. While both bodies have a substantive judging role to play as to the extent to which governments have complied with s.1, this judging takes place in the context of ongoing input from civil society, notably members of vulnerable and disadvantaged groups and the nongovernmental groups (NGOs) representing them, as well as from both the executive and legislative branches of government.

The Council has a set of "soft" functions to perform which collectively cast a constitutional spotlight on the rights in s.1 and ensure that policy-making decisions are made in as well-informed and educated a climate as possible. There are various axes of constitutional conversation involving the Council directly or indirectly. The Council is charged with educating the public as well as government officials (s.9(2)(d)). It may also hold inquiries as part of the process of establishing standards against which compliance with s.1 rights can be determined (s.9(2)(a)), and as part of the process of compiling the requisite data on the actual social and economic circumstances of those most requiring the Council's attention (s.9(2)(b)). In the course of these inquiries the Council can require the participation of members of the public and government (s.9(3)(a)). And in the context of these inquiries, the Council can require government to provide needed information and to report to the Council (ss.9(3)(b) and (c)).[16] All of these conversations may result in the Council "assess[ing] the level of compliance" of governments with s.1 (s.9(2)(c)), an open-ended evaluation which would be injected into general social and political debate. But the Council may also evaluate compliance by submitting "recommendations" to governments (s.9(2)(e)) which must be replied to within three months (s.9(4)). Significantly, there are no limits on the power of the Council to turn this recommendation-reply exchange into an ongoing dialogue. The Council also has the role of encouraging and mediating conversations with government from below and from above, so to speak. It has the duty to encourage governments to "engage in meaningful consultations" with NGOs representing the vulnerable and disadvantaged, in general (s.9(2)(f)) and in the specific context of the preparation of Canada's reports to international human rights bodies (s.9(5)(b)). With respect to these reports which the Council is empowered to assist in preparing (s.9(5)(a)), to dissent from by appending separate opinions to the final report (s.9(5)(c)), and to comment on before the international body if requested by that body (s.9(5)(d)), the Council must itself "actively consult" with such NGOs. Thus, the Council might be seen as a constitutionally designated interlocutor with the function of keeping the s.1 social rights in the mainstream of political and social discourse through the myriad of relationships it establishes with various actors.[17]   At one end, it is there to ensure that the voices from below are heard, so as to ensure that there is a constant dialectical interplay between general assessments of compliance with the s.1 social and economic rights and the concrete experience of those for whom these rights most matter. At the other end, the Council has some degree of symbiosis with a wealth of international activity, such as that of the Committee which oversees implementation of the International Covenant on Economic, Social and Cultural Rights. The overall effect is to make this hitherto rarefied and inaccessible process of international scrutiny more transparent, and to connect our constitutional conversation with another set of forums which are engaged in a "constructive dialogue" with the "state" of Canada.[18]

Other proposals circulating in the current debate go no further than recommending an entity vaguely resembling the Social Rights Council, although none has suggested in much detail what the functions of such a body would be. None of the other proposals take the idea of *claiming* rights seriously. By contrast, the ASC complements the Council with a Social Rights Tribunal. The Tribunal is a body which, like the Council, is best thought of in terms of its role as a constitutional interlocutor.[19] It shall have the duty to receive petitions alleging s.1 infringements, but its mandate is to scrutinize those petitions for the stories they tell about a systemic or otherwise significant deprivation of social rights (ss.10(1) and (2)). Thus, from the outset, the Tribunal process is geared to a form of structural analysis in which rights provide both the entry points and the source of concrete information (along with interventions from the Social Rights Council) necessary to evaluate the underlying sources of and extent of ill health, illiteracy, malnutrition and so on.

Several levels of dialogue may be noted within the Tribunal processes. First of all, there are s.10(4)(a) hearings that the Tribunal organizes to scrutinize those petitions that it has, as a preliminary matter, determined are indicative of systemic infringements of s. 1 rights. The hearings themselves, then, are the first occasion for a constitutional conversation. At the end of the hearings in question, the Tribunal may "issue decisions" as to whether a right has been violated (s.10(4)(b)). This moves the process into a second dialogue, namely that provided for in s.10(5). This dialogue is in essence a second-stage hearing on the appropriate remedy, in which the Tribunal hears the views of governments and petitioners as to "measures ... required" and "time ... required" (s.10(5)(a)). It is then contemplated that on the basis of this hearing, the Tribunal will "order that measures be taken ... within a specified period of time" (s.10(5)(b)) with this order making its way into the policy-making and legislative process (s.10(7)). It is important to note that, in appropriate situations, the Tribunal does not have to issue an order for measures under s.10(5)(b) but can instead, under s.10(6)(a), order the appropriate government to report back on the measures that the government has taken or proposes to take. Thus, the Tribunal may prolong the remedial dialogue, even after a s.10(5)(a) second-stage hearing. It might do this where it judges that further reflection is needed in light of the hearing, or where it simply judges politically that the issue in question is better served by the government making the first definitive proposal. Under s.10(6)(b), the Tribunal has the option of responding to the report ordered under s.10(6)(a) by issuing the order for the measures it initially declined to issue under s.10(5)(b) (which could involve endorsing the government's proposal or substituting its own view of appropriate measures) or by deciding to prolong the exchange on measures even further by issuing another s.10(6)(a) order to report back. Much like the recommendation-reply interchange involving the Council, there is no closure to the dialogue on appropriate measures, until the Tribunal decides to issue a s.10(5)(b) order for measures and send the question for final disposition in the legislative process. This is the third level of dialogue mentioned above. At this stage, the effect of the order is held in abeyance until the House of Commons or the relevant legislature has had a chance to consider the order; the delay could be a number of months, given that s.10(7)(a) requires the legislative body in question to have been sitting for a total of five weeks before the order comes into effect automatically.[20] In that time period, the legislature may override the order by a simple majority vote or, presumably, modify its scope.

The override mechanism has similarities to the s.33 "notwithstanding" clause in the *Charter of Rights and Freedoms* but is deliberately designed to avoid some of the failings of s.33. Under s.33, a legislature may override prospectively, by way of omnibus clauses applying to many pieces of legislation, and by making *pro forma* statements without indicating precisely which rights are being derogated from or which statutory provisions are at issue. The s.10(7)(a) override is an after-the-fact override which must be directed to a specific order emanating from a concrete set of facts and related hearings. What is more, the specific matter must be brought before Parliament, because of the default rule contained in s.10(7)(a) that the order goes into effect if the legislature does not act, rather than that the order's entry into force depends on whether it is endorsed by the legislature. These features of the override mechanism, along with the availability to the legislators of the record of scrutiny and dialogue within the Tribunal processes, make it likely that the debate envisaged by s.10(7)(a) will be more transparent and better informed than those which have generally accompanied the insertion of *Charter* notwithstanding clauses into statutes. All debates and votes would have to be conducted in the full glare of a constitutional spotlight.

The final point relates to the role of the courts. Section 10(8) is designed to prevent courts from entering the process too early. According to that provision, the Supreme Court of Canada is the only court capable of reviewing decisions and orders of the tribunal, and only on the grounds of a "*manifest* excess of jurisdiction."[21] Thus, in tandem with the Council, the Tribunal process is designed to get at systemic concerns and contribute to long-term remedies without having the judiciary tilt the process in undesirable or, at least, unpredictable directions. This is not to say that the courts might not over time see their way, in the spirit of institutional dialogue, to use the interdependence clauses in Part I to adjudicate individual claims by borrowing from the jurisprudence of the Tribunal and the softer assessments and recommendations of the Council.[22] Such a complementary judicial role would be appropriate, for instance, in urgent individual situations for which the Tribunal is ill-suited because of its focus on group-based infringements and because of the time-delay override clause, s.10(7). Judicial intervention would also be clearly called for to enforce the integrity of the process (for instance if a government refused to report as directed to the Tribunal), culminating in a role in enforcing any orders issuing from the Tribunal that have come into effect.[23]

The preceding account, in introducing the metaphor of rights as sites of dialogue, has set out one feature of what an alternative approach to rights might look like. We have also argued that such a metaphor points in the direction of processes of institutional dialogue similar to those contained in the ASC. We turn now to a second metaphor, which seeks to address what the substance of rights dialogue is and should be about. As will be seen, this metaphor, like the first, has an institutional corollary in that it focuses attention on the question of the interpretive vantage points which are or should be privileged by the composition and functioning of institutions, including those of the ASC.

Rights as relationship – a step toward substance

As we noted earlier, conversational metaphors can both mask and reinforce oppression.[24] We want, therefore, to introduce a second metaphor, *rights as relationships*, that not only complements the dialogue metaphor but also supplements it with critical bite – and helps to identify the critical potential of the ASC.

Our claim is that rights are best understood in terms of relationship. What rights do (and have always done) is structure relationships: of power, responsibility, trust, and obligation. This is as true of property (and its relations of power) and contract (defining the basic terms of exchange relations) as it is of more obvious areas like family law, which defines relations of responsibility, trust, and powers of control and decision making. Our argument is that this reality of rights as relationship should become the central focus of the concept itself, and thus the focus of all discussion of what should be treated as rights, how they should be enforced, and how they should be interpreted. It is really a matter of bringing to the foreground of our attention what has always been the background reality. We will handle all the problems of rights better if we focus on the kind of relationships that we actually want to foster, and on how different concepts and institutions will best contribute to that fostering.

Of course, saying this, does not itself define optimal relationships; hence it is only "a step toward substance." But at least the debate will take place in terms of why we think some patterns of human relationship are better than others, and what sort of rights will foster them. Suppose, for example, that we have some initial agreement about what we think optimal human autonomy would look like. We could then proceed beyond conclusory claims that autonomy requires individual rights to a close look at what really fosters the human capacity for autonomy and in what ways the relationships involved can be promoted and protected by legally enforced rights.

The ASC invites just this sort of inquiry. The clearest form of the invitation is the wording of s. 1(a), which refers to the "requirements for security and dignity of the person and for full social and economic participation in their communities and in Canadian society."[25] To determine what the rights in s. 1(a) are (and what would constitute violations of them), we have to ask what will make security, dignity and full participation possible. And the consistent focus on disadvantage suggests that until the relations of inequality are changed, security, dignity and full participation will not be possible for everyone.

Of course, the ASC does not *require* a relational approach to rights. (No interpretation is ever simply logically required.) It could be read as just stipulating material conditions each individual can lay claim to, independent of the network of relationships and memberships of which she is a part. But the repeated emphasis on disadvantage calls our attention to where people stand in relation to one another, and thus to what it would take to change those relations to make possible the well-being of all. This is the critical bite promised above: the focus on the patterns of relationship that must be changed or achieved to give effect to the goals of the ASC.

For example, if the system of social entitlements did not enable single mothers to get the kind of training and education allowing them to break free of the role of dependent, marginalized citizens, or did not enable a parent to stay home with a young child at a level of support sufficient for full social and political participation, then we would judge that system to fail the standards of the ASC. Where the choice has been made to provide benefits related to goods like food or shelter (whether in terms of in-kind provision or of financial entitlement sufficient to secure these goods in the market place), the quantity of the benefits alone could not tell us whether the standard has been met. The recognition that rights structure relations of equality and respect (or their opposites) would focus adjudicators' attention on the network of relations established or maintained by the system of benefits – and on whether that network was one within which people could be full participants in society.

The ASC avoids the use of the term "welfare" or "welfare rights." Apart from the stigma now associated with these terms, they have connotations of complacency with the current welfare state, including the image of the passive recipient of goods which are provided by the state at a level barely adequate to allow the recipient to survive, let alone flourish. In contrast, the ASC comes closer to projecting an image of aspirations to equal membership in Canadian society and of active involvement in realizing that membership. So, in phrasing the "umbrella" right in s.1 in terms of "everyone [having] an equal right to well-being," the focus is shifted from the particular institutionalized means associated with current welfare state arrangements to a more open-ended notion of a social state in which we are connected to each other in a network of more inclusive societal arrangements, the end result of which is a substantive state of affairs, "well-being."[26]

Section 1(a) is the subsection most expressive of the rights to well-being. With respect to every one of the goods expressly mentioned in that subsection, there are large sectors of Canadian society which do not have adequate independent financial resources to command these goods; nor are the various social benefit programs across the country generally adequate to redress the situation. So, it is this subsection, along with those work-related rights found in ss.1(d) and (e), which will provide the greatest focus in urging and pursuing social policies that attack the causes of poverty at the source, namely seriously unequal distribution of wealth, income and control of the conditions of work.[27]   The expression "standard of living that ensures" connotes more of a financial entitlement conception than a "services" conception, although state organization and provision of services is not precluded, and indeed, some of the listed goods (i.e., child care) will still be the avenue of choice for many social advocates. But, in general, the wording of s.1(a) suggests that the various "requirements for security and dignity of the person and for full social and economic participation in their [sic] communities and in Canadian society" (of which the list of goods are examples) are the benchmarks for determining whether a person's "standard of living" is adequate. There is nothing that requires the state to simply give in-kind goods and services to passive beneficiaries. Nor, however, does the wording of s.1 easily lend itself to arguments that government is justified in standing back and not doing anything to meet the requirement in question by way either of income redistribution or creation of a collective good. That is to say, the current situation of food banks and full or partial dependence on charity for many other services (i.e., battered women's shelters) is something that would have to be justified in terms of "security and dignity" and "full ... participation." What is more, interpretive arguments would have to contend with the overarching *telos* expressed in ss. 2, 4 and 5, notably "alleviating and eliminating social and economic disadvantage" (ss. 2 and 5).

The preceding point ties into the text's resistance to the tendency to frame rights entirely in terms of universal entitlement. One highly significant problem with legal rights, at least fundamental ones, is created when they are locked into a paradigm based on the universal attribution of rights. If "everyone" has the right to equality or to security of the person, then the needs and interests of particular oppressed and disadvantaged groups in society can never be (at least for very long) at the core of understandings of rights.[28]   Within all the discursive processes that would be set in motion by the ASC, there will be a textual touchstone for constantly contrasting understandings of the rights to well-being of "everyone" against the perspectives and needs of "members of [Canadian society's] most vulnerable and disadvantaged groups" (s.1). In other words, there is a presumptive privileging of those who we have good reason to believe have suffered and continue to suffer the greatest social and economic injustices in our society and, for that reason, must merit a priority of attention. This particularization of rights in the notion of "vulnerable and disadvantaged groups" returns to condition the functions of supervisory bodies under the ASC, the Council (see ss.9(2)(b) and 9(2)(f), and 9(5)(b)) and the Tribunal (see s.10(2)), and to be a feature of the criteria for the pool from which Council and Tribunal members will be drawn (see ss.9(9)(b)(iii) and 10(12)(b)(iii)). Thus, not only must the interests and perspectives of members of these sectors of society be heard within the various interpretive processes, but also they will be institutionalized under the criteria for representation on the Council and Tribunal.[29] This philosophy of representation derives from what are by now almost commonplace insights into the way in which particular interests and perspectives are systemically privileged when those with the authority to give meaning to rights are unrepresentative and unable to hear effectively the voices of all.

Finally, the ASC attempts to cap the statement of rights just discussed by implicitly querying two related separations that arguably are endemic to our liberal democracy. The first separation is the public–private split. Section 5 attempts to establish the rights in s.1 as an interpretive reference point for all facets of legal interpretation, by stating that, not only "[s]tatutes, regulations, policy, [and] practice," but also "the common law" is to be "interpreted and applied" consistently with s.1 and the "fundamental value" which underlies s.1, namely (again) "alleviating and eliminating social and economic disadvantage." The second separation is that between rights traditionally imagined as primarily negative (imposing duties of noninterference on government) and rights imagined as primarily positive (imposing duties on government to act to regulate private behaviour or to fulfil needs of members of society). If it may be said that the *Charter of Rights and Freedoms* has been conceptualized to date primarily in terms of negative rights, s.2 of the ASC encourages a more holistic interpretation of the *Charter of Rights and Freedoms* that is supportive of the rights contained in the ASC.[30]

The overall framework of an equal right to well-being in the context of responsibility for the most vulnerable and disadvantaged invites a structural, relational analysis that would take us beyond the social services model that some of the ASC's critics rightly question. If the basic rights are to well-being and full, equal membership in the community, then the provision of social services is only a possible means to be measured against the broader ends.

Concerns, Objections and Sites of Struggle

Perhaps the leading concern among those advocating a social charter
is that it not backfire so as to actually drain what modest empowering content there may be found in the *Charter* by creating a
jurisdictional excuse based on the notion that what is in one part of
the Constitution cannot be in another part as well.[31] The danger is
real.[32] Conceptualizing the rights contained in the two parts of the
Constitution as interdependent, or mutually reinforcing, is promoted
by an overlapping of language between ss. 7 and 15 of the *Charter*
and s.1 of the ASC, notably in the use of the words "equal" and
"security ... of the person" in the latter. If the ASC's values are not
incorporated into the *Charter*, at the very least the wording of s.2
should solidify the antidisadvantage principle that the Supreme Court
of Canada has evolved over the first decade of interpretation of the
s.1 "reasonable limits" clause of the *Charter*. This principle involves
a presumption against interpretations of *Charter* rights which would
thwart legislative initiatives designed to benefit disadvantaged
groups.[33] Interdependence is a two-way street, and the social rights
should be interpreted in light of the core values in the *Charter*, an
idea seemingly meant to be conveyed by s. 3 of the ASC: "Nothing
in s. 1 diminishes or limits the rights contained in the *Canadian Charter of Rights and Freedoms*." In our view, this interpretive clause suffers
from overly general wording and could actually undermine s.2. It
would be naive to think that there could never be conflict between
interpretations of the ASC and claims under the Charter. Section 2
might be said to stack the deck against certain kinds of *Charter* rights
claims (for instance, those advocating an employer's "liberty of the
[corporate] person" or "freedom of [corporate] association") that s.3
seems to state are not "diminish[ed] or limit[ed]" by s.1 of the ASC.
These potential conflicts, and the priorities that should guide their
resolution, need to addressed more directly through clearer wording
in s.3 – probably in terms that reiterate the "fundamental value" in
s.2 "of alleviating and eliminating social and economic disadvantage."

When interpreted to reinforce rather than undermine that
fundamental value, s.3 can be understood as stating that government
cannot in effect argue that a person must give up her *Charter* right in
return for respect of a social right or rights. For example, s.3 could
be a defence against a government arguing that, in exchange for a

certain social benefit, persons are entitled to less protection of their privacy rights (i.e., spot checks for an unreported income-providing "man in the house") or their mobility rights (i.e., residence in a province or city for a certain period before a social benefit will be accorded) or their right not to be subjected to cruel and unusual treatment (i.e., having names posted in public in order to discourage benefits claims and to encourage reporting on fraudulent claims) or their right not to engage in forced labour (e.g., workforce conditions on receipt of social assistance). These issues can be seen as examples of the sites of struggle that we offered as part of the sites of dialogue metaphor. The fact that the ASC cannot guarantee the outcome of such struggles is not an argument against it. The ASC *can* provide institutional forms in which the struggle can be carried out with a better chance for the disadvantaged to have their positions carry weight.

Another potential objection to the ASC is that it gives an unmanageably wide scope of authority to the Social Council and the Tribunal: the authority to inquire into anything in the Canadian political, economic, and social structure that impedes well-being and full membership. But the same is, in principle, true of the *Charter*; even the current conventions of focus on negative liberties would not prevent a far wider scope of inquiry under s. 15 than has been the practice so far. Only the (theoretically unsustainable) position that private suits at common law are outside the *Charter*'s scope prevents an inquiry into whether certain dimensions of property law or contract law are at odds with the "equal protection and benefit of the law."

In practice, what we can hope for from the ASC is a focus on the issues outlined, such as health, education, housing, and conditions of work, in ways that point to the deeper structures that shape any given social program. The structural, relational context of analysis can improve the political debate the ASC is designed to foster, and gradually shift public awareness, without its institutions laying claim to the entire political arena.

There is, however, a related objection which cannot be disposed of. The invitation to pay attention to structural problems rather than just the provision of social services opens the door to deep divisions over what sort of structural changes will actually best enhance well-being and full participation. Some advocate the virtues of the market on just those terms (usually with some scope for regulation and progressive taxation).[34] But we think that such debate cannot be foreclosed. The fact that many on the left and the right agree that a focus on social services turns attention away from underlying problems means that (in principle) there should be constructive debate on those terms. Clinging to an exclusive focus on entrenching social services as a rearguard action against destructive free-market ideology cannot really advance our capacity to ameliorate and eliminate disadvantage.[35] One of the virtues of the ASC is that it has the capacity to do more. But democratic debate cannot come with guarantees about outcome; it can only be structured in ways that give fair scope for the participation of the disadvantaged. And the ASC is an important step in this direction.

Conclusion: Texts that Matter

The ASC would not transform the deep structures of inequality in Canada. But it could offer the hope, not only of ameliorating the conditions of the disadvantaged, but of transforming the meaning of rights and of constitutionalism.

The initial debates around a social charter hit an impasse. Among those advocating a social charter there was no consensus about the appropriate role for the courts in its enforcement. Once a social charter was proposed, there was immediate resistance to the idea that the courts should adjudicate constitutional issues for which public spending was central. For many, the conclusion then seemed to follow that a social charter could not be enforceable; it would have to be merely a statement of principle. The ASC breaks through this impasse with an enforcement mechanism which is a viable, indeed preferable, alternative to the current court system. The democratic composition of the Tribunal, together with the ongoing dialogue it can create with legislatures, sets up a system of defining and defending rights that is itself democratic. The Tribunal does hold the legislatures accountable to the basic values of the social charter, but it does so in a way profoundly different from treating rights as trumps to legislative decisions. The ASC protects rights through a "dialogue of democratic accountability."[36] This provides a practical, and vitally necessary, alternative to the American conception of constitutional rights. The *Charter of Rights and Freedoms* had already taken important steps in that direction through the inclusion of s.1

and s.33. The ASC moves us still further toward treating rights not simply as limits to democratic outcomes, but the proper subject of democratic debate. The ASC institutionalizes rights as sites of dialogue and invites their interpretation in relational (and thus structural) terms. In doing so it goes beyond both of the competing American conventions of treating rights simply as instrumental to democracy[37] or as trumps to democratic decision making. It is thus an important step toward solving a very difficult, tripartite political problem: how to protect the rights essential to genuine democracy, how to make rights work as a protective check on democracy, and how to do both in a way that is democratically justifiable. In that sense, we think the ASC is a mere text that can matter in moving towards the values that both the advocates and many of the critics of the ASC share.

Endnotes

[*] The authors wish to thank Frank Cunningham as well as editors Joel Bakan and David Schneiderman for their comments. All standard caveats apply.

[1] For the first use of this metaphor, which has subsequently taken on a life of its own, see Ronald Dworkin, *Taking Rights Seriously* (Cambridge: Harvard University Press, 1978). For commentary, see Martha Minow, *Making All the Difference: Inclusion, Exclusion, and American Law* (Ithaca: Cornell University Press, 1990); Nedelsky, "Law, Boundaries, and The Bounded Self" (Spring 1990) 30 *Representations* 162; and Nedelsky, "Reconceiving Rights as Relationship" (1992) 30:2 Alta. Law Rev.

[2] See Nedelsky and Minow, *supra*, note 1.

[3] See for example Bakan, "What's Wrong with Social Rights?" (this volume).

[4] Dworkin, *supra*, note 2.

[5] For example, Wilson invokes the concept of "fences" in *R. v. Morgantaler*, [1988] 1 S.C.R. 30 at 164 even though she also says that the individual is not a totally independent entity, disconnected from society. In our view, she mixes her metaphors, invoking the notion of relationship, as well as that of fences. The strength of her opinion lies in the fact that it relies far more on the notion of relationship: "[Whether to have an abortion] is a decision that deeply reflects the way the woman thinks about herself and her relationships to others and to society at large." It is a decision "of the whole person." *Morgantaler*, at 171. See also Nedelsky, "Law, Boundaries, and the Bounded Self", *supra*, note 1.

[6] On the metaphorical structure of language and the need to be self-conscious about the metaphors we employ, see Nedelsky, *ibid.,* including her discussion of Johnston and Lakoff, *Metaphors We Live By* (Chicago: University of Chicago, 1980).

[7] See Dworkin, *supra,* note 1. And see Nedelsky, "Reconceiving Rights as Relationships", *supra,* note 1, for one critique of the Dworkinian notion of rights as trumps.

[8] The treatment of rights as rhetoric is part of both an old and a "new" rhetorical tradition. Amongst the classics are Cicero, *Topica*, trans. by H.M. Hubbell (Cambridge: Harvard University Press, 1960) and Aristotle, *Rhetoric* and *Topica*, trans by E.S. Forster (Cambridge: Harvard University Press, 1966). On the "New Rhetoric", see Chaim Perelman, *The New Rhetoric and the Humanities: Essays on Rhetoric and its Applications* (Dordrecht: D. Reidel Publishing Co., 1979) and Chaim Perelman, *Justice, Law and Argument* (Dordrecht: D. Reidel Publishing Co., 1980). See generally Friedrich Kratochwil, *Rules, norms and decisions: On the conditions of practical and legal reasoning in international relations and domestic affairs* (New York: Cambridge University Press, 1989).

[9] Fish, *Doing What Comes Naturally: Change, Rhetoric, and the Practice of Theory in Literary and Legal Studies,* (Durham, N.C.: Duke University Press, 1989) at 476.

[10] Martha Minow, "Interpreting Rights: An Essay for Robert Cover" (1987) 96 Yale L.J. 1860 at 1876.

[11] Ilmar Tammelo, *Treaty Interpretation and Practical Reason: Towards a General Theory of Legal Interpretation* (Sydney, Australia: The Law Book Company Ltd., 1967) at 46.

[12] Minow, "Interpreting Rights", *supra,* note 10 at 1894-5.

[13] This seems to be what lies behind Peter Goodrich's brilliant analysis of the need to supplement (not displace) a notion of law as rhetorics with a notion of law as (materialist) social discourse. Goodrich's project is to go beyond accepting and descriptive legal rhetorics as an elaboration of the "logic of legal values" and to "treat the rhetoric of law as a primary datum to be evaluated and appraised against the background of the institutional power and social relations of inequality, of superordination and subordination, that underpin that rhetoric and determine its semantic content." Peter Goodrich, *Legal Discourse: Studies in Linguistics, Rhetoric and Legal Analysis* (London, England: MacMillan Press, 1987) 124.

[14] See Joel Bakan, "What's Wrong with Social Rights?" (this volume).

[15] The complexities added by the federal structure of Canada will not be discussed in this chapter except to note that part of the ASC process will necessarily involve debate on jurisdictional issues, all the while noting that s.7 of the ASC places a "special role and responsibility to fund federal-provincial shared-cost programs" on the federal level of government.

16 Arguably, the amount of discretion accorded to the Council in the ASC proposal risks creating a gatekeeping mentality akin to that which has inflicted various provincial Human Rights Commissions across the country. Response from groups supporting the ASC in principle suggests the desirability of more explicit requirements for the Council to hold inquiries and require regular reports. For instance, a coalition of organizations representing the disabled has proposed adding a "barrier review" clause to the ASC draft which would read:

> Once every four years, Governments *shall* publish comprehensive reviews of the systemic barriers which exclude members of groups who have been found to be disadvantaged pursuant to section 15 of the Charter of Rights and Freedoms.

See Ad Hoc Committee of Disabled People on the Constitution, *Disabled People Moving Forward Together: Finding Our Place in the Constitution* (May 24, 1992) [emphasis added] [copy in possession of authors]. Compare to s.9(3)(c) of the ASC.

17 Again, however, it is arguable that the mediating role of the Council risks evolving into a gatekeeping or monopolizing role. As the text stands, only the Council, and not NGOs themselves, has the right to append separate opinions to international human rights reports and appear before international bodies; as well, the provision of a duty to consult NGOs falls directly on the Council but only indirectly on governments.

18 Such as the above mentioned Committee on Economic, Social and Cultural Rights, the Committee set up under the Convention on the Elimination of Discrimination Against Women or the monitoring bodies which operate within the International Labour Organization. On the conception of the international human rights reporting procedures as a "constructive dialogue", see, for example, Andrew Byrnes, "The 'Other' Human Rights Treaty Body: The Work of the Committee on the Elimination of Discrimination Against Women" (1989) 14 Yale J. of International Law 1 at 19-22. It is important to note that this is a metaphor which to date has had much more to do with diplomatic nicety than with the kinds of power-unveiling dialogic interchange that feminist scholarship has begun to call for. For a discussion of that scholarship, see Hester Lessard, "Relationship, Particularity, and Change: Reflections on *R. v. Morgentaler* and Feminist Approaches to Liberty" (1991) 36 McGill L.J. 263-307.

19 Note that there is one final axis of conversation in which the Council may engage but which was not mentioned in the preceding discussion, namely that with the Tribunal: see s.9(6) and s.10(9).

20 There is also provision in s.10(7)(b) for the terms of an order to be accepted without waiting for the legislature to begin sitting and then for five weeks to pass. This acceptance may be made by the "relevant government," which indicates that the only orders that may be accepted in

this way would be those which do not require legislative change but rather can be implemented through the executive's delegated decision-making powers.

[21] Section 10(8) [emphasis added].

[22] See ss. 2, 3 and 5, which are discussed, *infra* at text associated with notes 30 and 36-37.

[23] The judiciary is also clearly called on to enforce intergovernmental agreements and legislation related to s.1 rights: see s.6 of the ASC.

[24] See text at note 12 and the citation therein to Minow, "Interpreting Rights."

[25] We are not going to defend every feature of the rights framed in s.1 of the ASC. Indeed, we find some criticisms to have much validity, for example those of Joel Bakan and Hester Lessard contained in this volume with respect mainly to the right to health. We would be open to revisions of the text so that its resonance in the future politics of Canada is more likely to be progressive. Such revisions, in light of feedback of this nature including (at the most ideal) a constituent assembly to draft the final wording, were in fact part of the hope when this still preliminary text was released into the general debate.

We also think that, in keeping with the overall thrust of democratization in the ASC, "political" participation ought also to be included as a reference point for "standard of living" in s.1(a).

[26] The text is more or less successful in following through on that image in the nonexhaustive list of rights which derive from this umbrella right. The text appears to endorse a "services" conception of social rights in ss.1(b) and (c) by in essence entrenching quite general features of the current system of public provision of health and education services. This represents a pragmatic choice to recognize two sets of institutional baselines as an expression of what "we all" have achieved to date. The assumption is that such an approach is likely to marshall greater support for the overall package, especially in view of similarly phrased inclusions in both federal and Ontario New Democratic Party initiatives. There are also more principled reasons justifying such a strategic decision, not least of which is that it is often the wisest course to endorse a universal system, thereby putting all members of society in the same boat. This helps foster a situation in which the well-off have vested interests in humane and appropriate health care and quality education which are similar to those of the less socially powerful. Where gaps in health care or education begin to appear (whether in terms of basic access or quality), claims by those excluded can be more easily addressed by reference to the standards already enjoyed by others. That being said, it *is* admittedly still a weakness that these institutional features in ss.1(b) and (c) are protected, but not then explicitly linked to similar teleological statements as those that are found in s.1(a).

[27] Bakan, "What's Wrong with Social Rights?" (this volume).

[28] See Joel Bakan, "Constitutional Interpretation and Social Change: You Can't Always Get What You Want (Nor What You Need)" in Richard Devlin, ed., *Canadian Perspectives on Legal Theory* (Toronto: Emond Montgomery, 1991) (on underinclusiveness and overinclusiveness in rights discourse).

[29] Note s.9(8), which also links representation on the Social Rights Council to "demonstrated experience in the area of social and economic rights and a commitment to the objectives of the Social Charter" and s.10(10) according to which the Social Rights Tribunal "shall be made accessible to members of disadvantaged groups and their representative organizations by all reasonable means, including the provision of necessary funding by appropriate governments."

[30] Constitutional rights embedded within a conception of negative freedom project onto society an image of truncated personhood and an impoverished understanding of the positive bonds that connect us and that give meaning to our intermeshed individual and communal lives: Craig Scott, "The Interdependence and Permeability of Human Rights Norms: Towards a Partial Fusion of the International Human Rights Covenants", (1989) 27 Osgoode Hall L.J. 769-878; Craig Scott and Patrick Macklem, "Constitutional Ropes of Sand or Justiciable Guarantees? Social Rights in a Future South African Constitution", (1992) 141 U. Pennsylvania L. Rev.– [forthcoming].

That being said, it is crucial to note that the language of the *Charter of Rights and Freedoms* is still open to more holistic interpretations. See the discussion by Gwen Brodsky of the Supreme Court of Canada's still tentative approaches to s.7 and s.15 of the *Charter* in Brodsky, "Social Charter Issues" (this volume). And see Lessard, "Relationship, Particularity and Change," *supra*, note 21, esp. at 306, arguing for a new conception of s.7 "liberty" based on rights discourse being understood as "the language of democratic inter-relationships."

[31] See Brodsky, *ibid.*

[32] Lessons can be learned from the international human rights system and the existence of two different documents within both the United Nations system (the International Covenant on Civil and Political Rights and the International Covenant on Economic, Social and Cultural Rights) and the Council of Europe system (the European Convention on Human Rights and the European Social Charter). In cases involving trade union rights in both systems, governments argued strongly that separate textual locations of rights entailed a presumption against overlapping interpretations by the organs charged with interpretation of those rights. These arguments were neither explicitly endorsed nor explicitly refuted by either the European Court of Human Rights or the Human Rights Committee, but the results in the cases in question suggest that, at the least, the phrasing

of rights in the "social and economic rights instrument" can easily be seized on to put a ceiling on the interpretation of the rights in the "civil and political rights instrument": see Scott, "Interdependence and Permeability", *supra*, note 30 at 869-874 and J.G. Merrills, *The Development of International Law by the European Court of Human Rights* (Manchester: Manchester University Press, 1988) 202-204.

[33] See Ruth Colker, "Section 1, contextuality, and the anti-disadvantage principle" (1992) 47 U.T.L.J. 77. To the cases discussed by Colker should be added *Slaight Communications Inc.* v. *Davidson*, [1989] 1 S.C.R. 1038, esp. at 1051-2, 1056-7.

Apart from the general reaffirmation and solidification of the anti-disadvantage principle, it is well worth noting the way in which Chief Justice Dickson, for the majority, explicitly adopted a relational analysis of rights and their limits in *Slaight Communications*. In addressing the question of the freedom of expression of an employer with respect to an unjustly dismissed employee, Dickson C.J. made the unequal nature of the employment relationship pivotal to his analysis.

Quoting from Davies and Freedland, *Sir Otto Kahn-Freund's Labour and the Law* (3d ed.) (London: Skvens, 1983) at 18, he noted that such a relationship "is typically a relation between a bearer of power and one who is not a bearer of power ... [being] ... [i]n its inception ... an act of submission, in its operation... a condition of subordination'" (at 1051-2). He went on to state at p.1052:

> The courts must be ... concerned to avoid constitutionalizing inequalities of power in the workplace and between societal actors in general.... On the facts of this case, constitutionally protecting freedom of expression would be tantamount to condoning the continuation of an abuse of an already unequal relationship.

Dickson C.J. went on to interpret freedom of expression and its limits in light of a detailed analysis of the particular power relations involved in the case.

[34] See, for example, Joel Bakan's concern about arguments against regulation, rent control, socialized medicine, and collective bargaining in this volume.

[35] For example, there may be trade-offs in choosing the wording of the ASC. To the extent that the wording in s.1 (b) was changed to reflect Joel Bakan's and Hester Lessard's concern that the underlying causes of ill-health be addressed (rather than guarantees that health care will be provided once you get sick), it might have weakened easy claims to the provision of services at the same time that it opened debate to disagreements over structural causes and solutions. But, arguably, the debate would then be on the terms that matter.

[36] See Nedelsky, "Rights as Relationship," *supra*, note 1 for a fuller discussion of constitutionalism as a dialogue of democratic accountability.

[37] John Hart Ely, *Democracy and Distrust* (Cambridge: Harvard University Press, 1980) is the best-known form of this position.

6

What's Wrong with Social Rights?

Joel Bakan*

Ten years and several constitutional amendment processes ago, the *Canadian Charter of Rights and Freedoms* was entrenched in the Constitution. The event was widely celebrated by social activists and equality seeking groups. They saw the *Charter* as a vehicle for advancing social justice and equality. But events have not unfolded as expected. Courts have failed to breathe progressive life into the *Charter*, and they have made regressive decisions in its name.[1] Disappointment with the *Charter's* first ten years is mild, however, when compared to the profound despair on the left caused by regressive social and economic policies at all levels of government over the same period. For many, the solution to both problems is to entrench *another* charter, a social charter,[2] one that protects social or "positive" rights. They have embraced the idea as an answer to "Mulroneyism," and as a way to protect and recognize poor and disadvantaged people in the Constitution, and thus ensure their full citizenship.[3] A "social union," similar to the social covenant proposed in the Beaudoin-Dobbie *Report*, is part of the constitutional reform package for the

Referendum. Some of the authors in this volume find fault with it, and suggest alternatives. I will take a different tack. My argument is that the very idea of a social charter or union is flawed, and that, in any of its proposed forms, it is unlikely to do what those who support it want it to do. This is because social rights,[4] as they are articulated in social charter proposals, are too vague to guarantee anything of substance, do not touch the complicated causes of poverty and disadvantage, and their symbolic message is at best ambiguous.

Vagueness

All official or unofficial proposals for a social charter or covenant have this in common: the rights included, whatever their content, are couched in broad and general language, placing few constraints on whoever is responsible for their interpretation.[5] This means, among other things, that the progressive aspirations of social charter supporters may not find their way into authoritative interpretations of social rights.[6] Whether or not they do will depend upon who is doing the interpreting. Concepts such as "adequate social services and social benefits," "high quality education," "just and favourable working conditions," and "the highest attainable standard of physical and mental health"[7] are flexible enough to accommodate interpretations from different groups with conflicting interests, that are at once contradictory and plausible. Conservative governments and business groups will advance narrow interpretations of social rights, ones that impose limited duties on governments and private actors, and starkly oppose the broad interpretations of progressives.[8] There is no reason to believe progressive activists will be more likely (they may actually be less likely) to win these arguments about social policy under a social charter than in other political forums.

"So what?" one might respond. "A social charter may not get everything progressives want, but surely it is better than nothing." Maybe it is. I want to suggest, however, that it could be worse than nothing. The vagueness of social rights will allow conservative groups and governments to use a social charter *offensively*, as well as defensively, articulating their regressive aims and policies in terms of its provisions. For example, a government could defend ungenerous and regressive social policies by arguing that the policies meet social charter standards. The discourse of social rights is well suited for such arguments because of its "on–off" quality – either a right is breached, or it is not. Thus, a government might argue that its decision to lower or refuse to raise social assistance rates or minimum wages is justified because the current or new rate is equal to or higher than the minimum rate required by the social charter (as determined by an enforcement agency, or the government's own legal advisors). Ironically, along these lines, a social charter might actually *prompt* governments to cut spending and lower regulatory standards where the minimum levels determined to be acceptable under a social right are lower than the existing ones.

A government could also use social rights against public sector employees by defending back-to-work legislation for striking teachers or nurses on the ground that individuals are denied rights to education or health by strike related school and hospital closures, or rejecting wage demands by the same groups of employees on the ground that meeting them would require cutting education and health services in ways that would violate social rights.[9]

Business will also want to take advantage of a social charter, as it has of the *Charter*.[10] Where rights do not explicitly identify government as solely responsible for providing a service, business will be able to argue that certain kinds of economic and social regulations deny availability of that service to consumers, and thus violate a social right. Landlords could argue, for example, that rent controls or habitability standards violate the right to "adequate housing" because they induce capital flight from the market, and thereby have the effect of reducing rental housing stock. Doctors and pharmaceutical firms could argue that a right to the "highest attainable standard of health" is violated by legislative restrictions on the services and goods they can provide, and possibly, in the case of doctors, by the whole structure of socialized medicine.[11] Business will also be able to argue (as they have done successfully in Europe and in the southern United States) that a "right to work,"[12] or even a "right of access to employment opportunities,"[13] precludes union security provisions in legislation and collective agreements.

Social charter supporters recognize that social rights will not necessarily be interpreted progressively. This is why they are concerned about *who* should have authority to interpret and implement a social charter. Some argue that social rights should not be justiciable because judicial conservatism and unfamiliarity with "positive" rights would result in narrow and possibly regressive interpretations.[14] Others argue that if social rights are not justiciable they will be ineffective and not taken seriously.[15] Both arguments are partly right, though neither deals adequately with the legitimate concerns of the other. For our purpose, it is important to note that the anti-justiciability argument wrongly implies that difficulties raised by the vagueness of social rights are avoided by adopting nonjudicial enforcement mechanisms. While it may be true that the judiciary is more likely than other institutions to interpret social rights narrowly and regressively, it does not follow that such interpretations would be avoided in other forums. Whatever enforcement mechanism is chosen, narrow and even regressive interpretations of social rights will remain a possibility. Moreover, business and governments will be better equipped than social activists, in terms of access to the media, lawyers, lobbyists, experts and so on, to advance their interpretations of social rights in the judicial forum, and in the many forums of public opinion.

Social charter activists have used two techniques to limit the risk of regressive and ungenerous interpretations of social rights. First, they have specified in their draft proposals that only "vulnerable groups"[16] are protected by social rights, thus nominally barring powerful groups from using a social charter. But what is a "vulnerable group"? As Gwen Brodsky points out, this term will not necessarily keep out the wrong plaintiffs and allow in the right ones, and groups with regressive ambitions will always be able to find members of "vulnerable groups" to serve as plaintiffs, as they have done under the *Charter*.[17] Furthermore, even if complainants could be restricted to these groups, powerful and conservative governments and groups will still be able to make their narrow and regressive claims about social rights as respondents before the enforcement agency, and, more generally, in the media and public debate. A second strategy of social charter activists is to include language in their draft proposals that requires decision makers to consider the plight of poor and disadvantaged people. The Alternative Social Charter (ASC), for example, requires policies to be justified in terms of people's "security and dignity," and says that "alleviating and eliminating social and economic disadvantage" is its overarching *telos*.[18] I am sceptical about the effectiveness of this strategy in avoiding regressive uses of a social charter. The articulated aspirations of the ASC are neither denied by nor inconsistent with the rhetoric of the mainstream right. Indeed, security, dignity and elimination of poverty are often presented by the right as the *telos* for their favourite policies – free markets, competition, deregulation, and so on.[19]

Spending Priorities

A further difficulty with social rights (at least those requiring government spending) is that, assuming governments do not raise taxes, the revenue for their implementation will come out of existing budgets.[20] By necessity, an effective social charter will make some social goals priorities over others, and these priorities, not to mention the trade-offs they will require, may be undesirable from the perspective of many on the left and in social movements. Not all would agree, for example, that spending on health or education, each explicitly protected by a social right, is more important than spending on shelters for battered women, First Nations media and advocacy groups, foreign aid, or public broadcasting, to take just a few programs that might not come to be within the scope of social charter protection. While it is true that social spending always requires trade-offs, here, unlike other political contexts, the trade-offs will be frozen into constitutional law and placed outside the scope of political debate and change. This dynamic is often presented as part of the appeal of a social charter (it places certain things beyond the contingencies of politics), but whether it is progressive or not will depend upon *what* priorities are frozen into place, and from whose perspective the priorities are set. A solution to some of these difficulties would be for governments to raise taxes to pay for social rights implementation, thus avoiding cuts in other areas. However, it is unlikely that any agency will have jurisdiction to compel a government to raise taxes in the name of social rights, and it is also unlikely that governments will do so on their own. In any event, increased taxation to pay for social rights is not necessarily desirable. Governments may use regressive taxes (as they have been wont to do lately), and avoid any potentially redistributive effect of a social charter by forcing low income and poor people to pay for the implementation of their rights.

Treating Symptoms, Leaving Causes

Perhaps most importantly, social rights will not touch the real causes of poverty and other social ills. Social rights that impose obligations on governments to provide services,[21] even if they are effective in protecting and improving those services (a big "if"), are unlikely to have any effect on the social and economic relations that produce the need for those services in the first place. Despite all the rhetoric about Canada being a caring and compassionate society, the social welfare system in this country has done little to address issues of economic maldistribution, even at the worst end of the scale.[22] Universally provided services, like health and education, do not redistribute wealth (except perhaps to those who already have it), nor does the income security system taken as a whole.[23] Social assistance, the only program that is substantially progressive, provides an income that is only half the poverty-level income, allowing people quite literally to live in poverty rather than die from it. Universal access to state services may provide a safety net, but it has not transformed (nor will it transform) socially and legally enforced structures of economic inequality, and the unequal distribution of suffering and want they engender. Nor should we expect constitutionalizing universal access to such services through a social charter or covenant to change anything.

Health care provides a good example of the problem. The proposed social right to health in the Charlottetown Agreement, like that in other social charter and covenant drafts, imposes upon governments an obligation to ensure all Canadians have access to health care. It says nothing, however, about the social determinants of ill-health, particularly the unequal social relations that have much to do with why and to whom illness happens. The focus on access to *treatment* of illness occludes its social causes, constructing it as a biological or natural problem with scientific solutions. The right to health can thus be understood as reflecting and reinforcing the commonly held assumption that "... the determinants of health and illness are predominately biological, so that patterns of morbidity and mortality have little to do with the social and economic environment in which they occur."[24] In this view, illness is understood as something that just happens, rather than as the result of poverty and inequality; and universal access to medical services, not transformation of the social conditions that cause illness, is the focus of political action. The social constitution of illness, in particular the strong correlation between its distribution and that of wealth and income,[25] is obscured.

Poverty is the most extreme consequence of economic inequality, and poor people suffer substantially worse patterns of morbidity and mortality than others. However, the relationship between economic inequality and health applies not only to poor people but, more generally, to working-class people.[26] They too may suffer from inadequate nutrition and shelter because of low wages. Their jobs are often unsafe and unhealthy; they may unknowingly transport job related hazards to the places they live, and thus endanger those with whom they live.[27] The neighbourhoods in which they live tend to have higher rates of violent crime, accidents, industrial pollution and other health risks than do high-income neighbourhoods. Measures of morbidity and mortality demonstrate that low-income earners, along with poor people, are sicker, die earlier, and have higher infant mortality rates than those with higher incomes. The same is true of people who are unemployed and threatened with unemployment.[28] All of this has lead one medical commentator to state that "[i]f the health of the nation – the whole nation – is to improve then the distribution of the disposable income of its population needs to be made more equal. Establishing a classless society would not necessarily produce this outcome, although it would vastly increase the likelihood of doing so."[29]

Canada is very much a society of classes, intersected by gender and race inequalities, with a radically unequal distribution of wealth and income and correspondingly unequal levels of health in its people. This is neither natural nor inevitable. To the contrary, it is the product of state policy and the exploitative social and economic relations shaping such policy. While a classless society may not be on the cards, there are measures that would reduce ill-health in Canada by reducing health risks determined by class. These measures would have to go considerably beyond health and social service regimes and focus instead on transforming social relations that determine who gets sick and who stays healthy – unemployment, low income work, dangerous and unhealthy jobs, class-determined geographies of pollution, structures of employment that contradict child care needs, inadequate housing, and the ways these and other contributing factors intersect with unequal gender and race relations.[30]

Accessible and universal medical service may be necessary, but it will never be sufficient to ensure distribution of good health equally.[31] The most that can be hoped for from a social right to health services is the promotion of equal access to medical treatment, not equal access to good health.

The Symbolism of a Social Charter

Many supporters of a social charter concede some of the points I have raised. They are not sanguine about the concrete effects of a social charter, yet, they argue, the potential symbolic effects make it worthwhile. For them, a social charter would be a symbol of citizenship for economically disadvantaged and disempowered people; its absence would symbolize a denial of that citizenship.[32] As well, they point out, the symbolism of social rights would inspire and mobilize people to demand from governments fulfillment of social obligations. I find little comfort in these arguments and I am concerned that the symbolism of social rights might backfire badly. One of the symbolic effects of a social charter, for example, might be to obscure and go some way towards legitimating a reality of social wrongs. How many times does one hear that Canada is now a free and equal society *because* of the *Charter of Rights and Freedoms*, without any analysis of the actual impact of its provisions? Similar slippage is possible with social rights provisions. The ideals they articulate may be misinterpreted as descriptions of reality, and the effect may be to create an illusion of progressive social change when nothing has actually happened. Carol Smart has said that "the acquisition of rights in a given area may create the impression that a power difference has been resolved."[33] My concern is that social rights themselves may be understood as remedies for social inequality, and this will obfuscate the continuing need for social change.[34] "[R]ather than providing a springboard to the future [a social charter might thus] trap the country in the past."[35]

More specifically I am concerned about what social rights might symbolize, especially those related to social services.[36] I agree with social charter supporters that such rights symbolize something about citizenship, but what exactly is that "something"? I am afraid it may be a radically incomplete vision of citizenship, especially for poor and low-income people – a vision that portrays people as citizens so long as the state treats their poverty with income assistance and their illness with medical services. Citizenship, in other words, is about the state *treating* suffering. Unseen within this vision of citizenship is the fact the state supports and enforces the social relations largely responsible for the *production* of that suffering, *making* people poor and *making* them sick. The political and economic causes of poverty and illness are made invisible and irrelevant, implicitly relegated to the so-called "private" and de-politicized world of biology, individual choice and ability, family, and the market. Many social charter supporters have criticized civil and political rights as symbolizing an impoverished ideal of citizenship. Social rights, I want to suggest, can be understood in similar terms. Like civil and political rights, social rights to services are about how the state treats its subjects through state-sponsored programs. Though they call for state action rather than inaction – an important difference between social rights and civil and political rights – social rights, like civil and political rights, idealize citizenship in terms of how people are treated by the state, leaving unquestioned the causes of their exploitation and suffering in the so-called private world of social relations.

This is not a symbolic message people on the left should want to support. No doubt there is a need for social services, like health care or income security, but that is quite different from arguing that social services symbolize a progressive conception of citizenship. It is strange to say, for example, that poor and working-class people are citizens because they have access to universal, portable and publicly administered health care, when they live and work in conditions that will make them sicker and kill them sooner than their wealthier counterparts. The struggle for citizenship has to be about more than what the state should or should not do in terms of social services. It must challenge directly the exploitative relations of social life. As Meredeth Turshen has argued in relation to health: the

> first line of defense against ill health in a capitalist society
> is income-producing employment in a workplace that has
> a strong union to protect workers' health on the job and to
> negotiate benefits for them and their families.... The sec-
> ond line of defense, when the first has failed, is a welfare
> state to supply life's essentials – the food, clothing, shelter
> and medical care that [people] no longer have the income
> to purchase.[37]

The third, and most desperate, line of defense, in my view, is a social charter or union – especially one that glorifies the already "second-best" social welfare state as the achievement of full citizenship.

Conclusion

A social charter is not the solution to the profound, and profoundly worsening, economic and social inequality in Canada today, and it may end up being a part of the problem. Canada's New Democratic governments have each begun their terms by stating that "we have no money, we can't raise taxes, so we can't improve social programs, and we have to be careful not to regulate in ways that might promote capital flight." Do they, or anybody else, really think a social charter is going to solve their and our problems? Maybe I am naively optimistic, but I see an opportunity with the New Democratic Party in power in several provinces to break out of the reification of social services that is so much a part of our national culture, and to attack the causes of poverty and ill health with concrete social and economic policies aimed at reducing the unequal distribution of wealth and income, and reducing human suffering in Canada. Advocating a social charter is a much easier and politically safer strategy. It may prove to be an unfortunate diversion.

Endnotes

*   I would like to thank for their helpful comments on earlier drafts of this paper Paul Bakan, Rita Bakan, Susan Boyd, Harry Glasbeek, Marlee Kline, David Schneiderman and Claire Young.

1   See, for a discussion of how and why the Charter has not been progressively interpreted, J. Bakan, "Constitutional Interpretation and Social Change: You Can't Always Get What You Want (Nor What You Need)" (1991) 70 Can. Bar Rev. 307. For *contra* view of the role of rights strategies in social struggle (and the inspiration for the title of this piece) see Amy Bartholomew and Alan Hunt, "What's Wrong with Rights" (1990) 9 *Law & Inequality* 1.

2   The idea of a social charter was first officially proposed in Ontario's discussion paper of September, 1991: *A Canadian Social Charter: Making Our Shared Values Stronger* (Toronto: Ministry of Intergovernmental Affairs, 1991), though its impetus came from various community and antipoverty

groups. The federal NDP came up with their own social charter proposal as well. The Beaudoin-Dobbie Report endorsed the idea of a "social covenant" in *Report of the Special Joint Committee on a Renewed Canada* (Ottawa: Queen's Printer, 1992) and it is part of the July 2, 1992 and August 28, 1992 packages (see Appendix III and IV).

3   The idea of citizenship has been an important part of the social charter debate. It is used in two ways. First, there is the idea that Canadian citizenship requires common social standards across the country. This is how citizenship is linked to social rights in the Ontario discussion paper. (*Supra*, note 3.) Second, social rights are understood as ensuring the inclusion within the social and political community of poor and disadvantaged people. This understanding is more common among activists and antipoverty groups. It has its roots in post-WWII debates about citizenship and the social welfare state: see Bryan Turner, *Citizenship and Capitalism: The Debate Over Reformism* (London: Allen & Unwin, 1986). Also see P. Macklem and C. Scott, "Constitutional Ropes of Sand or Justiciable Guarantees? Social Rights in a New South African Constitution" (1992) 141 U. Pennsylvania L.Rev. – [forthcoming]: "A constitution containing only civil and political rights projects an image of truncated humanity. Symbolically, but still brutally, it excludes those segments of society for whom autonomy means little without the basic necessities of life." (at 37). But see: Malcolm Waters, "Citizenship and the Constitution of Structured Social Inequality" (1989) 30 Int'l J. of Comparative Sociology 159.

4   I use this term to describe the kind of abstract formulations of rights and commitments characteristic of current mainstream and alternative social charter proposals, and constitutional discourse more generally. I do not mean to include the more concrete and particular kinds of rights found in social and economic legislation and regulation. As will become clear, many of the difficulties with social rights flow from their abstract articulation, not from any problem inherent to regulating social relations through law.

5   For a discussion of vagueness (indeterminacy) in constitutional law, see J. Bakan, "Constitutional Arguments: Interpretation and Legitimacy in Canadian Constitutional Thought" (1989) 27 Osgoode Hall L.J. 123.

6   As I have argued in relation to the *Charter*, the fact that a right is broad enough to plausibly include a progressive interpretation indicates only that such an interpretation is possible, not that it is probable: see J. Bakan, *supra*, note 1.

7   These formulations are randomly taken from the various draft proposals, official and unofficial, that are currently in circulation.

8   The general conservative argument under the social charter will be, as Harry Glasbeek points out in this collection, that the surest route to better health, education and welfare is economic growth, and that is achieved through deregulation and cuts in spending and taxation. Social charter

supporters seem to forget that the "right" is not (openly) against social charter values. Conservative governments and business groups do not defend their calls for deregulation, privatization and low taxes by saying "we want to make more money," but rather by arguing that such moves will enhance our competitiveness and, eventually, our social welfare. Not surprisingly, powerful business organizations and mainstream media have indicated support for a social charter.

[9] Arguments about the negative effects of strikes and wage increases on consumers of public services are already made by governments during public sector labour disputes. Social rights would give these arguments an added bite by grounding them in the language of legal rights.

[10] See J. Bakan, *supra*, note 1 and M. Mandel, *The Charter of Rights and the Legalization of Politics in Canada* (Toronto: Wall & Thompson, 1989).

[11] These types of arguments would not be available for social rights which clearly impose corresponding obligations only on government, like the proposals relating to health care, education and income assistance in most of the official and unofficial drafts. This is clearly an advantage of that kind of right. The disadvantages are discussed *infra*.

[12] National Anti-Poverty Organization, *Draft Social Charter*, infra, note 13.

[13] National Anti-Poverty Organization, *Draft Social Charter* (March 27, 1992) s. 1(d).

[14] See, for example, the Ontario discussion paper, *supra*, note 2, at 16.

[15] See, for example, Martha Jackman, "Constitutional Rhetoric and Social Justice: Reflections on the Justiciability Debate" (this volume).

[16] See, for example, the discussion of the Alternative Social Charter in J. Nedelsky and C. Scott, "Constitutional Dialogue" (this volume).

[17] Gwen Brodsky, "Social Charter Issues" (this volume).

[18] See J. Nedelsky and C. Scott, *supra*, note 16.

[19] See, *supra*, note 7.

[20] This is a problem under the *Charter* as well. Interpretations of *Charter* rights may directly or indirectly require governments to spend money, though such situations are rare. With social rights to government services, they would be the norm.

[21] The most common formulation of social rights throughout the various official and unofficial drafts and proposals of social charters or covenants are in this form. They impose duties, or establish commitments, on governments to provide some service. This is true of the most recent social covenant proposal in the August 28, 1992 package.

[22] In 1984, the top 5% of wealth owners (assets minus debts) in Canada (>$300,000) owned 38% of all wealth in Canada, whereas the bottom 45% (<$30,000) owned 3.6% of all wealth in Canada. The wealthiest 5% thus owned ten times the wealth of the least wealthy 45%. The wealthiest 10%

owned just over 50% of total wealth. Statistics Canada, *The Distribution of Wealth in Canada, 1984* (Ottawa: Statistics Canada, Labour and Household Surveys Analysis Division, 1986). Similar distributions are apparent with respect to income. Here, the top 29% of income earners earn 43% of all income, the bottom 20% earn 4.7%. D. Ross and R. Shillington, *The Canadian Fact Book on Poverty, 1989* (Ottawa: Canada Council on Social Development, 1989) at 71-74. I do not think it is necessary to belabour the point – the distribution of income and wealth in Canada is radically unequal. It is, however, important to emphasise that these statistics do not account for exacerbation of the situation by unequal social relations of gender, race and colonialism.

23   A Report by D. Ross and R. Shillington (1986) for the Canadian Council on Social Development concludes:

> the overall distributional impact of the income security system...tends to be rather proportional. The bottom two, and top two quintiles each receive almost 40% of the total benefits, which is identical to their populations. The middle quintile receives a 20% share, also identical to its population share....

This is not surprising. Programs that provide a flat amount regardless of income (OAS, FA), or provide benefits proportional to income (pension plans, UIC, tax exemptions) cannot be expected to have a redistributive effect. The only truly redistributive programs are those that target low-income people (GIS/SA, social assistance, child tax credit). D. Ross and R. Shillington, "Background Documents on Income Security" in their *WIN: Work and Income in the 90's* (Ottawa: Canada Council on Social Development, 1986), 34-57.

24   L. Doyle, *The Political Economy of Health* (London: Pluto, 1979) at 12.

25   M. Rachlis and C. Kushner, *Second Opinion: What's Wrong with Canada's Health Care System* (Toronto: Collins, 1989) 178-186; L. Doyle, *Id.*; T. Delamothe, "Social Inequalities in Health" (1991) 303 *British Medical Journal* 1046; A. Baumeister, F. Kupstas, L. Klindworth, "The New Morbidity" (1991) 34 *American Behavioural Scientist* 468; M. Turshen, "The Struggle for Health" in R. Cherry *et al.*, eds., *The Imperiled Economy* (New York: The Union for Radical Political Economists, 1988). See also: National Council of Welfare, *Health, Health Care and Medicare* (Ottawa: Minister of Supply and Services, 1990) at 6.

26   It is important to recognize that economic and class inequality extends far beyond those who live below officially determined poverty lines. The almost exclusive focus on poverty in mainstream discourses about economic "class" can serve to obscure more pervasive problems. According to J. Westergaard and H. Resler, *Class in a Capitalist Society* (London: Heinemann, 1975) at 124:

> [E]ven when not intended that way, preoccupation with 'poverty' runs a constant risk of encouraging a distorted image of society. In that image 'the poor' – or a series of separate categories of poor – are singled out from the mass of wage earners from which they are recruited. And the division is ignored between the wage-earning class – in or out of poverty – and the secure though differentiated ranks of the 'middle and upper' classes.

[27] For example, women who live with men who work with vinyl chloride are twice as likely as other women to have miscarriages or stillborn births: R. Singh Bolaria, "Environment, Work and Illness," in R.S. Bolaria, ed., *Social Issues and Contradictions in Canadian Society* (Toronto: Harcourt and Brace, 1991).

[28] I. Mattiasson, F. Lindgarde, J.A. Nilsson, T. Theorell, "Threat of unemployment and cardiovascular risk factors: longitudinal study of quality of sleep and serum cholesterol concentrations in men threatened with redundancy" (1990) 301 *British Medical Journal* 461.

[29] Delamothe, *supra,* note 25 at 1050.

[30] Quebec seems to be taking the lead in this respect by bringing issues of unemployment, economic inequality, occupational health and safety, and others, within the rubric of provincial health policy. (See *The Globe & Mail* (16 June 1992) A1).

[31] According to one study, "the presence or absence of medical care accounts for only 10 per cent of the differences in mortality between different populations." See R.J. Haggerty, "The Limits of Medical Care" (1985) 313(6) *New England Journal of Medicine* 383.

[32] See P. Macklem and C. Scott, *supra,* note 3.

[33] Carol Smart, *Feminism and the Power of Law* (London: Routledge, 1989).

[34] The very attraction of rights, and the factor most apparent in popular discourses about them, is that in having a right, one has *something.* A right is "something to stand on." The right becomes the "thing," rather than the basis of a claim to it. In discussing "rights fetishism," Valerie Kerruish says: "What seems to happen is that these general rules somehow cast loose of their moorings as deliberately formulated standards for human action and float off to constitute a realm of the sacred." *Jurisprudence as Ideology* (London: Routledge, 1991) at 4. This kind of dynamic may be important for the mobilization of political struggle (on both the right and the left), or it may be co-opting, and promote complacency. To paraphrase Foucault, my suggestion is not that rights, including social rights, are necessarily bad, only that they are potentially dangerous.

[35] John Myles, "Constitutionalizing Social Rights" in H. Echenberg, A. Milner, J. Myles, L. Osberg, S. Phipps, J. Richards, W.B.P. Robson, eds., *A Social Charter for Canada: Perspectives on the Constitutional Entrenchment of Social Rights* (Toronto: C.D. Howe Institute, 1992) at 62.

[36] The arguments that follow are not applicable to social rights articulated in such a way as to encompass private as well as state actors. Nominally, these can be understood as imposing obligations on private actors and potentially challenging social relations of exploitation (though it is unlikely this will be the dominant understanding). One example is to articulate a right to health as a "right to the enjoyment of the highest attainable standard of physical and mental health," rather than a right to public health services. The disadvantage of this kind of formulation, however, is that it is broad enough to accommodate arguments like those discussed *supra*, note 10, and accompanying text.

[37] M. Turshen, *supra*, note 25, at 212. In adopting Turshen's words, I do not mean to suggest a "strong union" will ensure perfection, nor that other measures, such as stronger and better enforced employment standards, are not of equal importance. However, I do think that, in the context of contemporary North American capitalism, a strong union is a central means for ensuring that the interests of workers are protected.

7

Creation Stories: Social Rights and Canada's Social Contract

Hester Lessard

In this essay, I set out to examine the social rights debate. The lens through which I view the current discussions is the lens of feminism and, more generally, my commitment to a politics of anti-subordination.

The present moment in Canada is one in which there is at least an appearance of political restructuring underway, a moment of creative instability from which, presumably, a different alignment of power might emerge, perhaps even a democratization of power. The possibility of entrenched social rights seems very much a part of the promise of empowerment through constitutional renewal. Social rights are about redistributing wealth within the existing political structures. They promise to address basic material and social needs and to give some concrete content to the comparatively abstract and potentially empty guarantees of civil and political rights. Only the economically secure can afford to turn away from something that appears to provide an entitlement to food, shelter, health care, collective bargaining, education, and environmental protection. In addition, social rights lend moral and political authority to the claims of the most dispossessed within Canadian society.

However, a social charter can also be viewed as leaving the existing map of power-no power in place, and, by giving political and moral authority to that map, making us feel good about a social landscape that would recognize the most needy in our political economy without actually reworking the topography. From this latter perspective, the social charter leaves intact the liberal vision of a social contract between state and citizen, a contract which preserves a natural, and apparently necessary, division between public and private, and which presupposes the neutrality of the state. Indeed, the proposals for entrenched social rights emerging from the past year's constitutional discussions renegotiate the Canadian social contract in terms which would deepen and widen the public-private split and further entrench the myth of state neutrality. Meanwhile, what Carole Pateman calls the sexual contract remains invisible and submerged, and its terms remain essentially the same.[1] It is as if the liberal creation story is being re-enacted by the same actors with just a slightly different script.

In order to clarify my point, I will first examine the imagery of contract which often pervades discussions of constitution making, and which has been central in the current discussions of social rights. I will rely on the articulation of social rights contained in the Beaudoin-Dobbie *Report*[2] and the reformulation which appears in the Charlottetown Accord of August 1992. Second, I will argue that the new social contract contained in the Charlottetown Accord leaves intact the relations of subordination in two ways: first, by assuming a split between private interactions in the market and public responsibility for social well-being; and, second, by assuming the neutrality of the state in the provision of benefits. The first assumption gives shape to and sets the parameters for the constitutional rearrangement of Canadian economic and social life in the current proposals. The second assumption underlies the reliance on state provision of social benefits, which in turn flows from the presumed split between economic and social, private and public. In this section I will use the example of state complicity in sustaining the structures of sexual subordination through the regulation of reproductive health services, notwithstanding a statutory commitment to state provision of health benefits. In my view, to constitutionalize such a commitment in its present form will simply entrench the discrepancy between the official story of liberation and the actual story of oppression. Finally, I will suggest that a more extended constitutional strategy, one that places a social charter in the context of a larger goal of democratizing power in Canada, would more effectively dismantle the structures of subordination.

The Language of Contract and Constitution Making

As in most western democracies, women in Canada have engaged in long and difficult struggles to attain the status of legal persons with the formal rights of citizens. In many respects, these struggles, which we usually associate with 19th century western feminism, are not over. However, if we move beyond the realm of the formal and inquire into the ways in which the law effectively and indirectly entrenches and affirms sexual subordination – in domestic relations, employment relations and political participation – the story becomes depressingly repetitive. Carole Pateman explains the contradiction between the social reality of subordination and the official story of equality and full citizenship in terms of the sexual contract. In Pateman's view, the classical accounts of the origins of the legitimacy of the state in a social contract between naturally free individuals presumes that the basis of political right was originally in the relationship of father to son. However, Pateman argues that the paradigm of political right is not paternal power but the conjugal power of husbands over wives, which preceded the power of fathers over sons. Thus the liberal creation story of classical theory must be retold. It is a story about naturally free male individuals overthrowing the structures of paternal patriarchy and replacing them with the structures of fraternal patriarchy in which the male sex right is extended equally to all men. This is the sexual contract. Its terms are reflected in the experiences of women within relationships set in place by marriage, employment, prostitution, and surrogacy contracts.

Pateman's retelling of the familiar parable about the foundations of modern civil society can be faulted for ultimately speaking in images and archetypes that oversimplify and portray as universal, experiences which are complex, multi-layered, and socially differentiated. In effect, she replaces contract, as the archetype of freedom, with male-female relations, as the archetype of subordination.

Nevertheless, her unpacking of the myth of contract as the emblem of freedom remains a powerful critique of political authority and the use of consent to legitimate the exercise of both private and public power. It is particularly useful at this moment for Canadians when the imagery of constitutions as social contracts seems to have captured our political imaginations. Quebec and First Nations talk of being left out of, or never having consented to the constitutional arrangements of 1982 and the terms of the 1990 Meech Lake discussions. Likewise, the proposed entrenchment of social rights is described as a way of bringing economically marginalized groups within the terms of the renegotiated Canadian social contract of 1992. This language is powerful. When deployed by those who experience Canadian political and social life as outsiders, it lends authority to claims of belonging and to challenges to the legitimacy of the Canadian state as it is currently constituted. However, there has been very little reflection on the underlying assumption that consent, the central idea of contract, will transform social and political domination into social and political equality.

Pateman's central thesis is that contract is a device whereby freedom is transformed into subjection: civil subjection in the social contract, civil slavery in the employment contract, and sexual subordination in the marriage contract. She faults feminists and socialists alike for implicitly accepting the political meaning of contract as the paradigm of freedom and equality in their critiques of exploitive and unconscionable contracts. She observes:

> Contract theory is primarily about a way of creating social relationships constituted by subordination, not about exchange.... The new relationship is structured through time by a permanent exchange of obedience for protection.... The peculiarity of this exchange is that one party to the contract, who provides protection, has the right to determine how the other party will act to fulfill their side of the exchange.[3]

Pateman develops her thesis in the context of certain civil contracts in which an individual's property in the person – her mobility, her sexual integrity, her time and physical labour, comes under another party's control. This transformation into legitimate (because consented to) subordination is worth exploring further in the context of constitutions, which we still persist in thinking and talking about in contractual terms. Pateman's work urges us to question the extent to which the current proposals in Canada rely on a notion of constitutional bargaining and consent to ratify and legitimate a social system of subordination.

Much of the literature urging adoption of a social charter uses the imagery of contract uncritically. It also appears to accept that subjection in the private sphere of a globalized market is the "state of nature" from within which we must try to get the best contract or deal possible in terms of imposing public responsibility for social and economic protection. For example, the Ontario government's discussion paper, which in many respects launched the notion of social rights as a viable and necessary feature of a new constitution, describes such rights as "a strategy for ensuring that growing interprovincial and international economic competitive pressures do not become an excuse for weakening or abandoning our social contract."[4] Indeed, social rights are sometimes viewed as facilitative of economic integration and efficiency. The paper goes on to observe:

> National standards are very important in promoting the Canadian economic union. The efficiency of the Canadian economy is improved by the free movement of people, trade and investment across the country. Differing standards for health care or social assistance can act as a barrier to interprovincial labour mobility. By increasing labour mobility and strengthening the economic union, productivity, growth and international competitiveness are also strengthened.[5]

The idea that the growth of markets requires a level social playing-field in order to prevent social dumping and ensure fair competition also characterizes much of the writing by academic commentators. For example, Lars Osberg and Shelley Phipps, economists who write from a perspective which is sensitive to issues of equity and economic inequality, link a social charter not only to larger, freer, more globalized markets, but also to "a decreased role for the democratic process in restraining the impact of market forces."[6] This constraint on the efficacy of democratic politics is formally recognized in the Beaudoin-Dobbie *Report* in the recommendations to entrench the principle of free movement of "persons, goods, services, and capital" in a revised s. 121 of the *Constitution Act, 1867,* and to entrench property rights in the *Charter of Rights and Freedoms.* Osberg and Phipps also point out that the growth of the low-paying part time, temporary, and self-employed sector of the Canadian labour market in the last decade has rendered many of Canada's social insurance programs ineffective, especially for women who "constitute a large fraction of non-standard employment."[7] In their view, a constitutional reform that prohibits government interference in market transactions will only strengthen this trend, and thus social rights should be viewed as the necessary *quid pro quo* for giving up the democratic accountability of private power.

Osberg and Phipps are correct in pointing out that the entrenchment of free market principles without some sort of social buffer would deepen the economic divide between social groups, a divide that is neither race-neutral nor sex-neutral. However, because the price of protection is democratic rights, the reworked constitutional proposal can also be viewed as a very successful strategy to further marginalize socially subordinated groups in the political and economic decisions that affect their lives. In the next section, I propose to examine the way in which the specific terms of the constitutional contract recommended in the Beaudoin-Dobbie *Report,* and enshrined in the Charlottetown Accord, give rise to a renegotiated boundary between private oppression and public responsibility.

The Public-Private Split and the New Social Contract

Under the terms of the Charlottetown Accord, the proposed social charter will find its place in the Canadian Constitution as part of "The Social and Economic Union." The provisions announce a joint commitment by governments to five policy objectives: provision of health care which is "comprehensive, universal, portable, publicly administered and accessible," reasonable access to adequate "basic necessities," provision of high quality public education at the primary and secondary levels and reasonable access at post-secondary levels, protection of collective bargaining for workers, and "protecting, preserving and sustaining the integrity of the environment for present and future generations." These provisions are presented together with the economic union provisions which also commit government to five objectives: strengthening the economic union; free movement of persons, goods, services, and capital; full employment; ensuring a reasonable standard of living for all Canadians; and "ensuring sustainable and equitable development." The task of designing a mechanism for monitoring the implementation of these objectives is left to a future First Ministers' Conference. There is also a provision which states that the Social and Economic Union does do not "abrogate or derogate" from the rights in the Charter.

The Beaudoin-Dobbie *Report* articulated a hierarchy within which the social (understood in terms of individual need) was clearly secondary to the economic (understood in terms of transactional freedom). This was most evident in the proposed entrenchment of property rights in the *Charter*, and in the repetition of the commitment to "free movement of persons, goods, services and capital" in a revised s.121 of the Constitution. The primary reliance on free markets as the source and emblem of social prosperity is submerged more deeply in the Charlottetown Accord. Property rights have been removed from future constitutional agendas for the time being by Part IV of the Accord. However, the Charlottetown Accord commits First Ministers to implementing the principles relating to a Canadian Common Market contained in the political accord of August 28, 1992; as well, it gives First Ministers the authority to set up a dispute resolving mechanism in relation to those principles. The political accord is a document which is not being circulated with the draft of the Charlottetown Accord. The political accord reproduces much of the design for economic restructuring contained in the Beaudoin-Dobbie Report. It restates the free movement principle and reveals that the dispute resolving mechanism referred to in the Charlottetown Accord will report to First Ministers and will have a final and binding power to determine cases.

The political accord also sets out the key criteria for deciding cases. They are contained in two prohibitions: the first is against arbitrarily discriminatory trade barriers between provinces and territories, and the second is against trade barriers which impede the "efficient functioning of the Canadian economic union." The political accord suggests a number of exceptions and qualifications to the prohibitions in an attempt to preserve some scope for ameliorative and equalizing initiatives, and safety, equity, and fair trade practice measures. None of these principles or qualifications appear in the actual text of the Charlottetown Accord. However, ratification of the Charlottetown Accord would seem to impose a constitutional requirement on First Ministers to proceed with the blueprint in the political accord.

When one brings together all the pieces of the constitutional puzzle, what initially appeared as an aggregation of well-intentioned but vague commitments to socioeconomic harmony and well-being, is revealed as a much more focused set of constitutional priorities. A negative right against state intervention is created for economic actors. Meanwhile, the positive social obligations of governments are described, for the most part, in terms of process and form, i.e., reasonable accessibility, universality, and portability. To the extent that substantive entitlements are constitutionally conferred by the articulation of the five policy objectives, they are entitlements which Canadians already have under existing statutory regimes, such as primary and secondary education and a comprehensive public health care system.

A clearer sense of the violability of the social obligations emerges from s.26 of the Charlottetown Accord, which states that shared cost agreements under the Canada Assistance Plan cannot be unilaterally altered during a five-year term. After five years, agreements must be renewed by Parliament and the relevant provincial, territorial and aboriginal governments. This provides much more fiscal security for social welfare regimes than does the current arrangement. However, it offers an interesting contrast to the inviolability of the political accord's vision of a common market, the boundaries of which are not open to democratic renegotiation. In addition, complaints under the free movement principle contained in the political accord will be justiciable before a courtlike body, whereas the social obligations will be monitored by an undefined institution. Although I do not think justiciability would cure the defects in the proposal, I suggest that the institutional hierarchy reflects a normative hierarchy.

Finally, as in the Beaudoin-Dobbie *Report*, the separation of social and economic need from transactional freedom remains the foundational premise. It is governments, not private economic actors, which are responsible for the disadvantage that might flow from the distributional shock waves of integrated markets. Indeed, governments are obligated by the common market principle of "efficient functioning" to ensure that the enlarged private sphere remains insulated from social responsibility. Viewed in its full textual setting, the Social and Economic Union appears to have more to do with the consolidation rather than the democratization of social and economic privilege. This is accomplished through the device of an updated public-private split. Any gains that might be achieved in the restructuring of parliamentary institutions are effectively undermined by the entrenchment of a larger, stronger, less democratically accountable, and thus more "private" market. Even Osberg and Phipps seem to accept that, within this expanded sphere of freedom, an inevitable and natural relegation of female, immigrant, and aboriginal workers to the non-standard employment sector will occur. Furthermore, the *quid pro quo* for this renegotiated social contract is a set of social and economic entitlements which those workers already have and which already have been found sorely lacking. However, perhaps more important than the question of whether this might be a bad bargain, is the question of whether constitutions should be understood as bargains at all, especially as bargains in which political rights are given away in return for security, or as Pateman puts it, as a "permanent exchange of obedience for protection."[8]

The Myth of State Neutrality and the New Social Contract

In the foregoing sections, I attempted to sketch out the connection between the contractual language of bargaining and exchange and the assumption of a split between public responsibility and private economic interactions which underlies the classical liberal vision of social and political prosperity. In this section, I wish to examine a further way in which social rights, as they are currently conceived, suppress rather than respond to stories about disempowerment.

The promise of a set of social rights appears, at first glance, to challenge radically a central tenet of classical liberalism, namely state neutrality in the articulation of social goods. However, liberal democracies have for many years accepted the role of the state as the provider of social welfare. It is appropriate, but certainly not radical, for liberal democratic constitutions finally to reflect that reality. In addition, the commitment to welfare entitlements, far from transforming the state, has often provided a more extensive arena for the management and control of social groups under the guise of neutrality in the provision of social services and benefits. Thus, by constitutionally enshrining the welfare state, the myth of neutrality becomes less visible at the level of constitutional design, but more firmly embedded at the level of social interactions with the state. The experience of women in Canada with the provision of state-administered reproductive health services provides an example.

During the years when access to abortion in Canada took the form of a therapeutic exception to otherwise criminal behaviour, women were required by s. 251 of the *Criminal Code* to obtain permission for the procedure before a committee of doctors at an approved or accredited hospital. The committee was required to certify that the continuation of the pregnancy would endanger the life or health of the applicant. By constructing the abortion decision as one involving proper hospital facilities and medical diagnosis rather than moral or political concerns, Parliament was able to take the anti-choice stance required by conservative morality while at the same time maintaining neutrality towards the pro-choice exception. However, state neutrality was belied by the actual operation of s. 251. Women had extremely limited and difficult access to abortion services because of decisions by hospitals not to set up committees, varying interpretations of the criterion of danger to life or health, and the limited number of hospitals that qualified as approved or accredited hospitals. In addition, many of the health decisions by the committees were founded on a familial ideology which presumes that women are untrustworthy, especially with regard to their reproductive lives, and that the state through the delegated authority of doctors should maintain the natural hierarchy of sex-differentiated roles within the family. A survey of committee practices found that:

> More than two thirds (68%) of the hospitals surveyed by the Committee required the consent of the husband. A few hospitals required the consent of a husband from whom the woman was separated or divorced and the consent of the father where the women had never been married.[9]

The *Criminal Code* regime was struck down in *R. v. Morgentaler*[10] as a violation of s. 7 of the *Charter of Rights and Freedoms*. This was perceived as a victory for those who had argued for an understanding of abortion access in terms of women's social equality.

However, it soon emerged that what had been so dramatically swept away was only the most visible aspect of the complex arrangement of private and public interests that control reproductive decision making. Doctors and hospitals, both considered private actors with many of the same claims under the *Charter* to individual autonomy as their female patients, remained firmly in control of the delivery of abortion services.[11] Some hospital boards filled the vacuum left by *R. v. Morgentaler* by putting in place requirements which were more burdensome than those contained in s. 251 of the *Criminal Code*, or by refusing to provide abortion services at all.[12] Some professional medical associations formulated guidelines which restricted access.[13] Provincial governments also moved to limit access by imposing extra fees, requiring approval by anywhere from two to five doctors, de-insuring abortion services obtained within the province, de-insuring abortion services outside the province, and requiring abortions to be performed only in approved hospitals.[14] Without the obviously coercive presence of the criminal law, the complicity of the state in the continued disempowerment of women in the area of reproduction becomes increasingly difficult to identify. The subtle and complex intertwining of private and public power, and the resort to the neutral language of medical science or of budgetary restraint in recessionary times, renders the experience of oppression invisible or seemingly irrelevant to public debate and action. The official face of state involvement either takes the indirect forms of inaction and indifference, deference to the expertise of medical and health professionals, or deference to community autonomy, or the more direct form of the imposition of onerous but ostensibly neutral criteria for the delivery of abortion services.

In this situation, legal challenges to the apparently benevolent neutrality of the state must meet the narrow tests of a charge of colourability or of some other form of jurisdictional excess.[15] Shelley Gavigan describes this as jumping from "the 'criminal frying pan' only to be burned by the 'health care fire'."[16] For women seeking control over their reproductive lives, this has meant that the goal of establishing a network of abortion clinics continues to face deeply entrenched resistance. In some provinces, women still to have to travel thousands of miles, often at their own expense, in order to obtain safe abortions; in others, clinics face harassment and violent confrontations in order to keep their doors open.[17] In sum, women's

experience of a statutory entitlement to publicly funded health services demonstrates the limits of a conception of social rights which
presumes state neutrality and which operates within a contractarian
vision of political legitimacy. The proposed constitutionalization of
the main features of the existing scheme does not purport to address
those limits, but rather sanctifies them as constitutionally permis-
sible.

Conclusion: Changing Our Constitutional Visions

As Shelley Gavigan has written, "it will continue to be critical for
feminists, activists and academics together, to explore and expand
the social right to health care envisioned by the early advocates of
comprehensive health care."[18] In order to do so, we need, first of all,
to expose what the Social Covenant is not. For instance, with regard
to health care, it is not an entitlement to reproductive services. Nor
is it protection against forced obstetrical intervention. Nor is it an
obligation to take lower technology procedures out of the medical
sphere in order to ensure culturally sensitive and women-centred
health services. Nor is it a commitment to address the systemic
causes of "bad health." Nor is it an assurance that if one is a poor
woman or a lesbian woman or a First Nations woman, one's children
will not be "rescued" and placed in socially approved families. Second, we need to create political space for a wide range of groups in
order to develop an understanding of what a social right to health
care entails in socially specific terms. Third, we need to place the
social rights strategy in the context of a broader challenge to the
ostensibly neutral constitutional structures which enforce a system of
privileging and marginalization. Finally, we need to challenge the
assumption that constitutions are social contracts, negotiated from
within the state of nature. Within the present creation story, the
naturalization of globalized markets underpins and informs the terms
of the new constitutional bargain. Ultimately, the contractarian vision of political organization constitutes what Pateman describes as
an exchange of obedience for protection, an acceptance of civil subjection in return for security. Good health should signify
empowerment. It should not signify an inducement to accept a "natural" state of chronic political disempowerment.

Endnotes

1   C. Pateman, *The Sexual Contract* (Stanford: Stanford University Press, 1988).

2   Special Joint Committee on of the Senate and House of Commons on a Renewed Canada, *Report* (Ottawa: Queen's Printer, 1992) (Co-chairs: G.-A. Beaudoin and D. Dobbie).

3   *Ibid.* at 58-59.

4   Ontario, *A Canadian Social Charter: Making Our Shared Values Stronger* (Discussion Paper) (Toronto: Ministry of Intergovernmental Affairs, September 1991).

5   *Ibid.* at 7-8.

6   L. Osberg and S. Phipps, "A Social Charter for Canada?", in J. McCallum, ed., *A Social Charter for Canada?* (Toronto: C.D. Howe Institute, 1992).

7   *Ibid.* at 12.

8   C. Pateman, *supra*, note 1.

9   S. Gavigan, "Morgentaler and Beyond", in Brodie et al., eds, *The Politics of Abortion* (Toronto: Oxford University Press, 1992) 117-146 at 134, writing about the Badgeley Committee's Report.

10 [1988] 1 S.C.R. 30.

11 The status of hospitals as private rather than public actors was established in *Stoffman* v. *Vancouver General Hospital*, [1990] 3 S.C.R. 483.

12 For example, on February 27, 1991, the Dauphin board of directors voted to ban all abortions except those where the patient was obviously threatened by death because of the pregnancy. The policy was subsequently endorsed at a shareholders' meeting attended by more than 1000 people who had acquired voting rights by paying a $3.00 fee. Although there were complaints that the vote had been stacked by anti-choice activists brought in from outside the community, there are no residency requirements for becoming a voting shareholder. E. Christie, "Abortion Access after *R.* v. *Morgentaler*," August 11, 1992, unpublished draft on file with the author. By way of contrast, in British Columbia, the Minister of Health recently ordered the Vernon Jubilee Hospital to provide abortions. The hospital board then voted to delay compliance, claiming political interference in hospital business. The stand-off finally ended when eight members of the sixteen member board quit. E. Christie, *ibid.*

13 For example, until this past March when it voted to approve clinic abortions, the Saskatchewan College of Physicians and Surgeons bylaws stated that abortions require the approval of one additional physician or an approved counselling service and can only be performed in an accredited hospital. The College has also refused to give Dr. Morgentaler a licence to practice in the province. E. Christie, *ibid.*

[14] S. Gavigan, *supra*, note 9 at 140-145. See also "Across Canada" (Spring 1992) *Pro-Choice News* at 5-6.

[15] For example, in *R. v. Morgentaler*, (1991) 83 D.L.R. (4th) 8, lv. to appeal to S.C.C. granted Nov. 14, 1991, the Nova Scotia Court of Appeal found that the Nova Scotia legislature, under the guise of preventing the privatization of medical services and maintaining a high standard of health care, had attempted to prohibit abortion clinics and restrict access to abortion, thereby trenching on Parliament's exclusive jurisdiction over criminal law. However, Freeman J.A for the majority held that the Nova Scotia legislature clearly has the power to enact such a law dealing with abortion so long as the primary aim is health care matters. In *Lexogest Inc. v. Man. A-G* (12 June 1992) [unreported decision] (Man. Q.B.) provincial regulations which de-insure clinic abortions were challenged on a number of grounds. The Court found that the Lieutenant-Governor-in-Council had no statutory authority to exclude services from coverage on the basis of location. The constitutional authority of the legislature to do so, however, seemed to be assumed.

[16] S. Gavigan, *supra*, note 9 at 145.

[17] "Across Canada" (Spring 1992) *Pro-Choice News* 5 at 5-6 summarizes incidents of vandalism and bomb threats at clinics across Canada in recent months, as well as the abortion policies of various provincial governments such as Newfoundland, New Brunswick, and Prince Edward Island which force women to seek out-of-province abortions.

[18] S. Gavigan, *supra*, note 9 at 145.

8

The Social Charter:
Poor Politics for the Poor

Harry Glasbeek

The Social Charter is seen as an antidote to the business agenda of the federal Conservative party, an agenda which is attempting to unleash the full fury of market forces. The public sector is under attack and all political barriers to profit-seeking are being demolished. This agenda began to be played out by the Mulroney government when it initiated the free trade deal. It was reflected in the *"CAP"* on transfer payments to the provinces and it is to be made concrete by the new constitutional proposals. Social programs are being diluted or abrogated; the rich are paying less tax and the mobility of capital has been enhanced. Both organized labour and working people everywhere are facing a fierce onslaught. A riposte is needed. Some have seen the social charter as part of the answer. This is a snare and a delusion.

From Charter to Charter – An Unnatural Progression

The same people who made the argument that the social charter is needed were very strong supporters of the *Charter of Rights and*

Freedoms when it was first put on the bargaining table. It was claimed that, as an enforceable statement of values and aspirations, the *Charter* would help emancipate Canadians and, by increasing their political power, give them a stronger voice in their society. What was not anticipated by these people was how well the wealthy and the corporate sectors would fare under the *Charter of Rights and Freedoms*. In particular, these sectors have had remarkable success in inhibiting state regulation and thereby increasing their power *vis-à-vis* the disadvantaged and the workers of this country. It has become harder for the state to investigate the crimes of corporations, and business has become freer to fund political parties than it ever has been, something which has turned out to be a boon for them and helped the Mulroney forces win the free trade election. Business is as free to advertise toilet paper as we are to speak on street corners about the need for child care, perhaps freer, and business has managed to get the Supreme Court of Canada to say that the rights to strike and to picket, labour's way of speaking, are not fundamental rights. Further, the state has inhibited itself. It fears potential *Charter* challenges by business against any action it might take on behalf of people. The legal claim the state fears is that any progressive policy will be said, by *Charter* interpretation, to affect adversely the private property interests of the wealthy.

These are bold assertions. *Charter* proponents would reject them or, at least, want them nuanced. But they cannot negate one proposition; indeed, it has been implicit in their argument for a social charter. It is that the politics of constitutional litigation have not been able to stop the onslaught of private power in this era of economic restructuring. It is somewhat paradoxical, then, that the social charter movement has been accepted by Canadians in large part because they are being offered another charter. The continued (and, in my view, unwarranted) celebration of the *Charter of Rights and Freedoms* has given it a great deal of prestige and legitimacy. Yet an effective social charter is one which would counter the *Charter of Rights and Freedoms* directly. This is so because the latter emphasizes the individual's rights *vis-à-vis* the state, whereas a social charter is meant to enforce the collective needs of the people.

The Social Charter as a Set of Constitutionally Enforceable Rights

An effective social charter would require governments to attack the distribution of private wealth and to reduce the prerogatives of management. The *Charter of Rights and Freedoms* sets out to defend individual rights against the state, not against other individuals. For its purposes, the wealth and class of individuals are of no significance. As a consequence, its application ignores existing inequality created by private ordering and makes it difficult for the state to redress these imbalances. If the judiciary were to be charged with applying both the *Charter of Rights and Freedoms* and the social charter, there would at best be incoherence: at worst, a complete enfeeblement of the social charter. If social charter proponents had won the right to have the values and aspirations of the *Charter of Rights and Freedoms* read subject to those of the social charter, there would have been a crisis of legitimacy for the judiciary. This is so because historically the judiciary is wedded to the idea of supporting individual rather than collective rights. In any event, it was unlikely that social charter proponents would have been able to get that kind of provision in the Constitution. For one thing, it questions the supremacy of the *Charter of Rights and Freedoms* in the constitutional hierarchy, something taken for granted by all the national parties involved in constitutional deal making. It truly was most unlikely that a provision could have been included in any new Constitution which would have derogated from the *Charter of Rights and Freedoms*. In fact, the contrary seems to be true, as many now seek to dilute the "notwithstanding" clause in order to enhance the weight of the *Charter of Rights and Freedoms*.

Avoiding these problems by having the social charter enforced by an alternative tribunal raises another kind of difficulty. Is it likely that a social charter tribunal could have the legitimacy of the judiciary which interprets the *Charter of Rights and Freedoms*? This seems implausible. In the result, any kind of contradictions which arose would lead to an undermining of the interpretation of social rights.

In short, the effective enforcement of a social charter has ideological and practical problems to overcome. To overcome them requires different politics than any that have been presented at the constitutional table.

Social Charter Rights as a Solemn Declaration

If the social charter is seen as a way of saying through a constitution that social rights should be respected in Canada, it amounts to no more than a lofty statement of aspirations. Yet this is the position promoted both by the Ontario New Democratic Party and the federal NDP, and it is reflected in the Charlottetown Accord. It avoids the necessity of having to specify what quantity and quality of social rights should be provided and, of course, it avoids the difficulties of enforceability set out above. But, if a social charter enshrined in a constitution is not enforceable, all it can possibly do is give those people who want the protection of the state for social rights some political ammunition to fire at the politicians who are not fulfilling their commitments.

The Social Charter in the Context of Constitutional Deal Making in Canada

In the last two hectic days before the Beaudoin-Dobbie *Report* was concluded, both the Liberals and the NDP resisted signing it because they had not got what they wanted. Eventually, the NDP felt that it could sign because it had "forced" a social charter of the kind it wanted on the Conservative members of the Beaudoin-Dobbie Committee. What had been called the "hijacking" of the federal Conservative Party's constitutional agenda was claimed to have been completed.

At one of the weekend constitutional conferences for "ordinary" Canadians, there was much debate about the fact that the socialist left and their allies had forced a new agenda on the Conservatives by attacking the corporate sector's proposals for economic union and substituting for them a demand for a social charter. But there never was any hijacking. The people who effectively introduced the idea of inserting a social charter were those well-known "lefties," Tom Kierans and Claude Castonguay. This was something of a surprise, because when the social charter was first put on the political agenda by the Ontario NDP, it was considered just another hoary left-wing proposal which would go nowhere, especially since it was met coldly by the Quebec government. All of a sudden, red Tories were able to support it. In short order, the proposal also got support from Joe Clark, *The Globe and Mail* and *The Financial Post*, amongst others. At first blush, then, the suggestion that getting a social charter inserted into the constitutional proposals is evidence of a successful hijacking operation by the undifferentiated left, is unpersuasive. But there is more to this sad story than this.

The social charter offered by the Beaudoin-Dobbie *Report*, and ultimately incorporated into the constitutional accord of August 1992, took the form of an addition to the existing section 36 of the Constitution. Currently, section 36 of the *Constitution Act, 1982*, provides that the federal and provincial governments are committed to promote equal opportunities for the well-being of Canadians, to further economic development to reduce disparity in opportunity, and to provide essential public services of reasonable quality to all Canadians. That section is legally unenforceable. It obviously has never put any pressure on politicians who were seen as not living up to its requirements. How else could one explain the success of the attack by the federal government, and by all other governments in Canada, on the social welfare system?

The new s. 36.1 proposal provides that all Canadian governments are committed to fostering comprehensive universal, portable, publicly administered and accessible health care, adequate social services and social benefits, high quality education, the right of workers to organize and to bargain collectively, and the integrity of the environment. But, the text of the accord goes on to say, this is but a statement of goals for governments, not a set of enforceable requirements. To help put pressure on the political governments of the day to strive to achieve these goals, the Beaudoin-Dobbie *Report* recommended a monitoring body, like the Auditor-General of Canada or the Human Rights Commission (which reports on voluntary compliance systems in the federal sphere, to no effect whatsoever). At any rate, there is no particular reason why a political government should act in any particular way to prove that it is committed to, say, adequate social services, as required by s. 36.1. For instance, an NDP government might well want to increase taxes and redistribute them to provide social services; a Conservative government might say that it will put itself in a position to provide better social services by taxing the rich less, leading to more investment which, in turn, will lead to a better tax base and more economic welfare, both lessening the need for provision of welfare by the government and allowing it to provide more bountifully for the few who need it. Both plans of action could be said to be manifestations of a sincere commitment to the s. 36.1 goal.

Why on earth, then, are the forces of the NDP and their supporters so sure that they managed to score a victory? Their argument is that they were able to spike the economic union proposal of the federal government and replace it with their unenforceable social charter (which is now to be called, and this is meaningful, a "social union").

In September 1991, the federal government offered as part of its proposals for constitution making a new section 91A. It was widely perceived to be a central plank of the government's evident design to create a liberalized, trade-led economy with which no government should interfere. Section 91A proposed to grant the federal government a power to legislate "in relation to any matter that it declares to be for the efficient functioning of the economic union." Although the federal government was to be granted this jurisdiction, any laws that passed under the aegis of the proposed s. 91A would have required the approval of the governments of at least seven provinces which, together, had more than 50% of the population. The implementation of this economic union was to be governed by a new Council of the Federation. The whole proposal, but especially the establishment of an overseeing body, drew everybody's (and particularly Quebec's) fire and attention. The proposal was said to have been torpedoed by the same band of hijackers who put the social charter on the agenda. But what do we find in s. 36.2 of the Beaudoin-Dobbie *Report*? There is a provision that the governments of Canada will be committed to work co-operatively to strengthen the economic union, to ensure the mobility of persons, goods, services, and capital, to pursue the goal of full employment and to ensure that all Canadians have a reasonable standard of living. The essence of the hated economic union clause, without the offending Council of the Federation, is stuck in the same section as that vanguard of revolution, the social charter. The authors of the Beaudoin-Dobbie Report, undoubtedly aware of the irony, stated in the Report that governments ought to be careful how they pursue the goals of economic laissez-faire found in s. 36.2. In line with this proposal, it (like s. 36.1, the social covenant) is not to be enforceable.

Inasmuch as the entrenchment of the social union in the constitution may provide ideological support for progressive forces trying

to get social welfare out of governments, the installation of the economic union type of clause in exactly the same section, with exactly
the same enforcement mechanism (that is, a monitoring device which
will hold subsequent parliaments to account), gives an equal ideological amount of support to antiprogressive forces. But that is not
all that happened as a result of the Beaudoin-Dobbie *Report*. The
original federal proposals also had contained a proposition to extend
s. 121 of the existing Constitution. As it stands, it requires that "all
articles of the growth, produce, or manufacture of any of the provinces shall, from and after the union, be admitted free into each of
the other provinces." The interpretation and application of s. 121 has
been limited to inhibit those provincial economic measures which act
as barriers between provinces. It has not been used at all to catch
those measures which regulate the market-place *within* the provinces.
As a consequence, Ottawa's pro-liberal trade policy makers proposed,
in September 1991, that there should be a "common market" clause
which would guarantee the free movement of persons, goods, services and capital within, as well as across, provincial and territorial
boundaries. Any laws or practices which acted as a restriction on
mobility were to be of no force or effect. There were to be some
narrowly confined exceptions which space does not permit setting
out here. What is significant is the sense of the provision, which had
been urged by both right-wing intellectual gatekeepers and big business lobby groups.[1] That is, the intent was to expand s. 121 and to
make it truly enforceable. From this perspective, the proposed s.
91A was just a cherry on top of the ice cream. The amended s. 121
was to be where the real liberalized trade proposal was to be found.
The Beaudoin-Dobbie *Report* kept this, the real common market clause,
intact. Not only that, but it was to be enforceable, unlike the social
covenant or the economic union clause found in ss. 36.1 and .2. It
was to be enforced by a newly created tribunal, staffed by experts –
economic experts, no doubt. For those who know the economic
profession and have seen what has happened under the Free Trade
Agreement, this bodes ill. The proposal has since been shelved for
consideration at a future first ministers' conference. But there was
agreement in August 1992 to proceed with a political accord adopting many of the Beaudoin-Dobbie recommendations on the common
market.[2]

The real agenda of the corporate sector was retained in the Beaudoin-Dobbie constitutional proposals. From this perspective, granting the "left" an unenforceable social covenant while protesting that the "left" has won, seems like a macabre joke. As if to emphasize that business had given up nothing, the Beaudoin-Dobbie *Report* also proposed that private property be an entrenched right in the new Constitution. While the proposal ultimately was dropped, the signals being given by the Conservative forces in this country are unmistakeable: business should be free to do with its property as it likes and where it likes, without any restrictions whatsoever.

Fighting Where it Counts

The arguments for a social charter type of instrument came as a response to the political and economic restructuring which is occurring. This also was the case in Europe, where the trade union movement sought this kind of protection from the anticipated ravages of liberalized economic policies. There, too, workers have failed (thus far) to get what they need. The importance of pinpointing how these arguments arise is that the movement for a social charter is not a movement for transformation, but rather one which accepts the inevitability of the changing relations of production and which seeks some mediation of their impact. What follows from this is not that people should not fight for the rights which would have been included in any decent social charter. But they should not be involved in trying to obtain them in an unenforceable form in a setting where much is being given away at the same time. Sadly, this is what has happened in the current round of constitutional deal making in Canada. Progressive people would better spend their energy to establish basic social welfare rights, including an extended right to strike, by fighting for them where they can get them in a concrete form. They can get these rights through direct legislative action. Each government in Canada is constitutionally equipped to give them all the rights that would be included in any social charter found in the Constitution. Moreover, the rights can be enforced by these governments. Further, every jurisdiction in this country is on the record as being committed to all the goals which are found in the social covenant, whether it be universal schooling, health care, collective bargaining, minimum wages, set levels of occupational health and safety, equal pay for work of equal value, and so forth. Why not get these institutions, rights and conditions improved and enforced? Here the irony of the NDP gambit becomes apparent. If the NDP in Ontario really feels that all these things are vital, why does it not act on them? If it does not do so (as it has not, for example, with the right to strike) because business is too powerful, we have come full circle. Why does the Ontario government engage in politics which *beg* for these social and political rights from its malevolent opposition? Is it satisfied with an unenforceable social covenant because it has accepted that it cannot get any more?

The ideals of a social charter remain attractive. In practice, it may turn out that a social charter becomes a way for government and others to avoid having to engage in transformative politics.

Endnotes

[1] For a very precise accounting of the huge range of activities which the right-wing academic ideologues and the business groups would like to see subjected to the new s. 121, see David Schneiderman, "The Market and the Constitution" in D. Cameron and M. Smith, eds., *Constitutional Politics* (Toronto: James Lorimer and Co., 1992) at 61-63. Most interesting is his finding that the pan-Canadian common market proposal has had the support of not only Conservatives everywhere, but also of the federal Liberals' present leader, and of the Allaire Report. There seems to be unity amongst big business everywhere. This is *the* real problem for working people who, along with their other divisions, struggle with constitutional fragmentation.

[2] It has run into flak for all sorts of reasons, one of them being that the prohibition is not wide enough and effective enough to satisfy business and the Mulroney government agenda of deregulation.

9

The Constitutional Politics of Poverty

David Schneiderman

Introduction

The speed at which the social charter proposal has become part of the landscape of current constitutional politics is surprising. By contrast, many proposals central to accommodation in this round of reform have taken years of political ripening before gaining substantive fruition. Why is it that we are talking about a social charter at this time, and what is it that we mean when we talk about it?

There is little doubt that the intersection of the crisis in fiscal federalism with the dynamics of constitutional reform has precipitated much of this discussion. This intersection is not simply coincidental. Cutbacks in federal transfer payments, together with decreasing provincial revenues and increasing costs in the delivery of social programs, reinforced provincial demands for greater control over the establishment and maintenance of national programs (through the spending power), and power sharing, even devolution, in a number of key social and economic areas (such as labour market training).

Social charter advocates, such as Ontario Premier Bob Rae, have employed the social charter card as a tactic so as to continue, or at least halt the erosion of, federal commitments to provincial social programs. At the same time, the social charter has appeared as a salve to the laissez-faire economic strategy of constitutionalizing the Canadian common market. It also has the apparent virtue of being a symbol of national cohesion at a time when economic and social pressures, both global and continental, continue to erode Canadians' sense that they are more sharing and caring than their southern neighbours. The social charter initiative should be seen, therefore, as reactive and crisis managing, and as a largely symbolic endeavour.

The discussion also has created space for others who have appeared more recently on the constitutional scene. The emergence of this space, of the type described by Jane Jenson, has provided an opening "in the universe of political discourse to demonstrate alternative meaning systems and to institute alternative practices."[1] These nongovernmental actors, particularly from the anti-poverty movement, were prepared to push for substantive social rights in the Constitution, not only as a palliative to the erosion of the welfare state, but also as a means to advance the substantive interests of the disadvantaged. Despite this opening, the anti-poverty movement did not attempt to address the origins of the current crisis. They did not offer coherent alternatives to the neo-conservative economic agenda, an agenda which was advanced in the federal government's 1991 constitutional proposals. Nor did they address issues such as continentalization and globalization, and the pressures they have placed upon the social welfare state. The left's response, both from within the anti-poverty movement and the New Democratic Party, largely has been inchoate and reactive.

My aim here is to document this opening and thereby place in context the social charter debate. This will necessitate a brief discussion, firstly, of the fiscal pressure which provincial governments face, and which has precipitated talk about the social charter. I will then discuss how governments and political elites have responded recently to these pressures and then, lastly, how the anti-poverty movement joined into the debate. My focus will be to document the struggle taking place in Canada over defining the direction of social policy. It then should be evident that the debate has been blunted by the apparent willingness of all of the actors, both from the left and from the right, to agree to terms which sustain the conservative economic agenda of the Mulroney government.

Fiscal Federalism Follies

In 1982, Canadians enshrined, in part, in s.36 of the *Constitution Act, 1982*: (1) an inter-governmental commitment to "providing essential public services of reasonable quality to all Canadians"; and (2) a federal commitment "to the principle of making equalization payments to ensure that provincial governments have sufficient revenues to provide reasonably comparable levels of public services at reasonably comparable levels of taxation." The section is somewhat discordant, committing both levels of government to providing "essential public services of reasonable quality" and the federal government to paying for "reasonably comparable levels of public services." In the face of declining commitments to funding social programs, "reasonably comparable levels" of services may not be equivalent to public services of "reasonable quality." In any event, the federal government is committed constitutionally to financing essential and reasonably comparable levels of public services, despite any province's tax base or "fiscal capacity."

Much of what the federal government does is redistribute wealth. Some of that has been accomplished through personal transfers to citizens directly through such programs as unemployment insurance, family allowances, old age security and the Canada Pension Plan.[2] As a result of divided jurisdictions, where provinces have constitutional responsibility for social services but not sufficient revenue, much of those transfers occur through federal pooling of revenue – much of it under the control of the federal government, some of it collected on behalf of provincial governments through "tax rental agreements" – with transfers to provinces which do not have the fiscal capacity to meet national standards.

Federal transfers to the provinces, in order to maintain those standards, occur in three major ways.[3] First, there are "equalization" payments to the "have-not" provinces, calculated so as to bring all provincial revenues up to the standard of five "representative" provinces. These transfers are not tied to any particular services: governments are free to spend this money in ways they see fit. The Atlantic provinces and the midwest (Saskatchewan and Manitoba) rely particularly on these transfers. Other transfers, under the federal government's spending power, are tied to the delivery of certain "essential public services." Despite the constitutional commitment to ensuring that essential public services of reasonable quality are provided, it is in these areas particularly that the federal government has been eroding its financial commitment.

Under the Established Programs Financing Act (EPF), federal revenue is transferred to provincial governments for the purposes of health and postsecondary education. These payments are provided partly in federal cash transfers and partly by way of tax points to the provinces. Through this program, the federal government sets "national standards"[4] in the delivery of health services. For example, it coerces provincial governments to meet the five requirements, all enshrined in the Canada Health Act, that provincial plans be comprehensive, universal, portable, accessible, and publicly administered. Even then, these standards in the main are not vigorously enforced or, at least, have been unevenly enforced.[5] There remains an ever-widening degree of discretion in provincial governments. The government of Saskatchewan, for example, has considered removing coverage for all therapeutic abortions within that province at the same time that the province of British Columbia has mandated the same service be provided in all provincial hospitals.[6]

Although the federal financial commitment has been steadily eroding, even long before the Tories came to power,[7] the 1990 federal budget was one in a series of frontal assaults on the social welfare state. In the name of federal deficit reduction, it was announced that there would be a freeze on EPF transfers for two years, after which payments would be increased at the rate of the GNP minus three percentage points. The 1991 budget extended the freeze for yet another year, to the end of the 1994-1995 fiscal year. Federal savings would be substantial and the federal cash portion of EPF transfers to all of the provinces likely would disappear, according to the National Welfare Council, by the year 2009-2010.[8] With the disappearance of federal cash transfers, the financial stick for enforcing national standards enshrined in the Canada Health Act would snap.

A similar trend has occurred in regard to another federal transfer which ensures essential public services of reasonable quality: the Canada Assistance Plan. Here, the federal government provides 50% of the funding required to deliver a number of social welfare programs. Under the plan, provinces are obliged, in part, to provide financial assistance to those residents who qualify under a "needs" test. As the National Council of Welfare reports, "the amounts provided by provincial welfare programs for basic assistance are usually far below the poverty line."[9] Again, as of the 1990 federal budget, CAP transfers to the three "have" provinces (Alberta, British Columbia, and Ontario) have been limited to 5% a year for two years. In the 1991 budget, that ceiling was extended for yet another year to fiscal year 1994-1995. Increases in welfare costs beyond 5% per year would have to be picked up by those provinces, either by raising taxes or by running greater deficits. Together with the federal government's entry into direct taxation through the Goods and Services Tax, the "haves," who have the greatest numbers of Canadians on social assistance, are left with few options. And it is clear how this federal government feels about provinces engaging in deficit financing of provincial programs.[10] This unambiguous assault on fiscal transfers was resisted fiercely, first by unsuccessful litigation,[11] and then by the Premier of Ontario together with western Premiers, who indicated that no constitutional accommodation would be forthcoming without settling the fiscal issue.

Ontario's Proposal: Bread or Circus?

It was in response to the federal government's unilateral cutbacks in EPF and CAP that Ontario Premier Bob Rae put the social charter on the map. He insisted that any future constitutional negotiations would have to consider the province's financial needs to meet these social welfare commitments. These needs could be accommodated, suggested Rae, by a social charter entrenched in the Canadian Constitution. If those social commitments were entrenched in the constitution, argued Rae, "it [would allow] us to be more flexible on the question of the division of powers in terms of how we deliver programs."[12] The government of Ontario, in its discussion paper *A Canadian Social Charter: Making Our Shared Values Stronger*, made even more clear that the government's concern was with meeting provincial financial commitments under current national shared-cost programs. The social charter would "ensure that the social policy infrastructure cannot be destroyed for reasons of short-sighted political expedience or misguided economic theory."[13] The entrenchment of a constitutional commitment to social programs would have the effect, the Ontario government hoped, of ensuring that the federal government could never again entrap provincial governments into making social commitments without the continued commitment of federal dollars.[14] It was not a visionary document but a pragmatic response to preserving social programs at a time when they were under extreme fiscal and international pressures.

As the Ontario proposal concerned itself with federal transfer payments, and only indirectly with individual entitlements, the discussion paper proposed a variety of entrenchment mechanisms designed to meet *provincial* needs. Justiciable social rights are frowned upon: "To be consistent with the requirements of our democratic tradition, general principles [in a social charter] should not transfer the obligation to develop and implement social policy from governments to the courts."[15] Such "rights," rather, while entrenched, should continue to be subject to mechanisms of political enforcement. The Ontario paper foresaw public participation only in the drafting of the charter and, perhaps, in a nonbinding review mechanism.[16] The federal government recoiled initially at the concept: it was noticeably absent from the federal government's package of 28 proposals in September 1991.

It became clear, however, that Ontario's demands would have to be taken seriously if constitututional reform was to proceed through the provincial negotiation stage. At the same time, constitutional strategists became aware that their proposal to constitutionalize the common market in proposed amendments to s.121 would attract hostile opposition from the same quarters which had opposed the free trade deal and from those who supported the New Democrats provincially in a number of recent electoral victories. As a result, in the fall of 1991, federal signals were broadcast that a social charter could become part of the package: "Ottawa to float concept of constitutional 'social charter'" the headlines read.[17] The continuing emphasis on a social charter to meet provincial needs persisted in the follow-up recommendations of the federal New Democratic Party and the government of the province of Ontario. The federal New Democrats proposed entrenching a social charter in s.36 of the *Constitution Act, 1982*. These new commitments would be monitored by a permanent standing committee of a reformed Senate. One had difficulty seeing, however, provinces being amenable to snooping by federal senators in areas of provincial purview. The Ontario government also proposed an amendment to s.36, together with an independent commission to oversee and monitor implementation of the social charter.

It was not surprising, then, when the Special Joint Committee on the Constitution (Beaudoin-Dobbie) in March 1992 proposed a non-justiciable social charter of provincial needs, with an intergovernmental enforcement mechanism, twinned with an economic covenant. But we are jumping ahead of ourselves, for the next phase of the struggle over interpreting needs took place in the context of the federal conferences on the renewal of Canada.

Efficiency or Equity or Both?

A large number of the 28 federal proposals tabled in 1991 concerned "enhancement" of the economic union. This would be achieved, in part, by constitutionalizing the "free movement" of persons (corporations), services and capital, a new federal power to manage the economic union, and devices for co-ordinating budgetary practices and policies. The "free movement" or common market clause, in particular, could have significant effects on provincial governments' abilities to regulate the market place.[18]

The emphasis on enhancing the economic union seemed odd, considering that the Canadian federation, on the whole, was an efficiently functioning economic union with very few remaining barriers to interprovincial trade.[19] If these barriers were negligible in terms of cost to consumers and as a percentage of the Gross Domestic Product, why push at this time for a constitutional amendment? It was reasonable to suspect that the aim of the proposal was to constitutionally disable provincial governments from acting, so as to protect and regulate local markets in a wide variety of ways. This, of course, was exactly the aim of the federal government and its allies, such as the Business Council on National Issues and the Canadian Manufacturing Association, who had seen nontariff barriers between provinces as an obstacle to the efficient unimpeded operation of the market.[20]

As well, the common market proposal had the advantage of speaking a language that the new political and economic elites in Quebec could understand. The common market proposals potentially could lure these elites back into the federalist fold.[21]

It appeared as if the free trade debate would be playing itself out again, but this time in the context of the "Canada round" of constitutional reform. Given the instability of the whole constitutional reform process, federal strategists likely realized that this opposition somehow would have to be neutralized. Some ideological assistance came to be provided by the proponents of the common market.

If proposals for the efficient functioning of the economic union were constitutionally feasible, some economists argued, then "equity" issues also would have to be addressed. Robin Boadway, for example, argued that if we are aiming to increase the "economic pie" by freeing up the market, those collective gains somehow will be redistributed.[22] The equity role of government, therefore, is to divide up and allocate those gains. And there are good efficiency arguments in favour of enhancing that equity role. In the absence of fiscal transfers, argued the Economic Council of Canada, provinces will compete to attract capital by offering "net fiscal benefits" (fewer taxes, regulatory policies, government services) not available in other provinces.[23] This can lead to "excessive mobility" and inefficiencies in trade and labour mobility not dependent on the market. As well, this competition can lead to a spiralling downward harmonization of social programs. National standards, therefore, help to enhance the economic union.

Ideally, then, the federal fiscal system with national standards in place would treat otherwise identical persons living in different provinces the same. While proposals to constitutionalize the common market assists in that direction, constitutionalized equity proposals would also assist. We moved significantly in that direction in 1982, argued Norrie, Boadway and Osberg, when we entrenched equalization commitments in s.36 in the *Constitution Act, 1982*, but that project remains incomplete. They proposed, therefore, entrenching a guarantee of equality of opportunity as well as a guarantee to a minimum standard of living.[24] Constitutionalizing *both* efficiency and equity could advance the goals of the economic union, paste over opposition to the common market, and gain the allegiance of the Ontario government. And, even Ontario had acknowledged that these social commitments would not have the force of rights claimable by individuals before courts of law (justiciable rights); rather, they simply could be commitments in the same way as equalization is a non-justiciable (so it is claimed) commitment enshrined in the constitution.

It was only after the Calgary constitutional conference on institutional reform that the social charter project was fully embraced by fiscal conservatives. This came, significantly, at a time when pressures were being generated for democratic reform of central institutions. Concerted political action by women attending the Calgary conference – to place equality in the forefront of representational concerns – was somewhat successful. Women from across the country made known their opposition to the traditional terms of the debate over institutional reform, which continued to exclude the meaningful participation of over one-half of the population. At the subsequent conference on economic union in Montreal, this movement was derailed, largely by the insurgent issue of the social charter.[25] The catalysts were two apparently uncoordinated speeches delivered the very first day of the conference. Senator Claude Castonguay, formerly co-chair of the Joint Parliamentary Committee on the Constitution, declared himself in favour of the social charter concept.[26] Tom Kierans, president of the co-host for the conference, the C.D. Howe Institute, declared himself similarly in favour.[27] As "Canadians fear that increased economic efficiency will lead to the loss of the 'fundamental equity principles that bind us,'" Kierans declared, the social charter should be taken seriously.[28] The social charter continued to be raised in the subsequent two conferences, and the issue of women's equality mostly disappeared from the constitutional landscape.

It was also at the Montreal conference that the proposed federal power to provide for the "efficient functioning of the economic union" was abandoned. The proposed power could have been exercised only with the consent of seven provinces representing at least 50% of the Canadian population. While the clause, as proposed by the federal government, had the potential of being used to curtail provincial intiatives that acted as barriers to trade essentially through the doctrine of paramountcy, it also had the potential of acting as an important lever in the national economy. This was a role which had long been advocated by economic nationalists. The social charter indirectly had the effect of sidetracking what could have been an important new instrument for national economic planning.

The resulting version of the social covenant found in the Beaudoin-Dobbie *Report* and, ultimately, in the Charlottetown Accord, like its companion, the economic covenant, would be a series of proposed constitutional commitments whose realization would be monitored by a new intergovernmental mechanism. Unlike the proposals by Boadway and others, the covenant would not be justiciable.

The Antipoverty Response

This distinction was not lost on the antipoverty network which developed proposals for a draft social charter. In opposition to the New Democratic versions, and the follow-up Beaudoin-Dobbie recommendation, antipoverty groups formed caucuses and drafted a comprehensive charter which returned to the proposals of Boadway, Norrie and Osberg (full equity together with full efficiency).[29] The social charter proposals were drafted in the language of equal opportunity: standards of living which would ensure full social and economic participation, accessible post-secondary education, and access to employment opportunities were included. Two bodies were to be created: the Social Rights Council would evaluate compliance with those commitments; the Social Rights Tribunal would hear petitions alleging infringements of the charter from individuals and groups.

The antipoverty draft, whose drafters were cognizant of the critique that social rights could be invoked by the wrong persons, endowed as the "main purpose" of the Social Rights Tribunal the consideration of petitions "alleging infringements that are systemic or that have significant impact on vulnerable or disadvantaged groups and their members." Concerns about the antidemocratic nature of justiciable rights discourse were addressed partially, as compliance orders made by the Tribunal could be overridden by a simple majority in the House of Commons or relevant legislative assembly. As well, the federal government's special role in the redistributive state was reinforced.[30]

But many concerns remained, including the constitutionalization of the inadequate status quo. While legislators could be clobbered over the head by the negative findings of the Social Rights Tribunal should they depart from the status quo norm, this hardly addressed the concerns of the disadvantaged regarding the inadequacies of the present system. While the social charter might, in theory, prevent things from getting worse, they likely would get no better. But would it prevent things from getting worse?

The movement from a national economy to a "globalized" one, together with an emphasis on deficit reduction, places severe fiscal constraints on governments to redistribute wealth. In particular, there has been a marked decrease in the economic pool from which social services are financed together with an increasing unwillingness on the part of the public to continue financing fully the welfare state. These financial pressures being placed on the provinces leave them with few options. National standards likely will continue to spiral downward. Would the antipoverty social charter have had the effect of curtailing this trend? Probably not.

The economic restructuring associated with what Robert Cox calls "hyper-liberalism"[31] means the end of the Keynesian alliance between government, business, and labour.[32] No longer is development of a domestic market for domestically produced goods and services a priority. In the age of globalization, concerns about the inefficiencies of the redistributive state are secondary to the removal of the state from important areas of economic and social control. Hence, the push to constitutionalize the common market and constitutionally disable governments from acting, so as to distort the operation of the market. There is a corresponding push, as well, to harmonize social programs downward. As North American free-trade talks move to fruition, pressure will be even greater. One would not expect the Canadian social charter to play any significant role in this context.

Conclusion: Pastures Greener or Meaner?

The social charter proposal exhibited a general intellectual malaise regarding political-economic issues. This was in spite of the opening that the social charter debate gave to progressive forces to craft a reply to the fiscal conservatism of the Mulroney years. The Canadian public, having caught out the intellectual limits of its political elites, invited others to provide more creative and interesting solutions to the Canadian federation's impasse. But, as Jim Silver has noted, we have failed to stimulate new thinking: "Neoconservatives have seized upon the opportunities created by the [constitutional] crises as a means of advancing their ideological project; the same crises have elicited only ideological confusion from the political and intellectual left."[33] This is a mournful state of affairs, at the least, for no other reason than that a variety of constitutional options have been overlooked, if not foreclosed.

While the motives of antipoverty activists who were pushing for a justiciable social charter to aid the disadvantaged were laudable, this group appeared willing to accept the ideological causes for the fiscal retrenchment, which could be found, in part, in the federal government's 1991 constitutional proposals. It is not my intention here to outline a solution to the economic challenges facing Canada's social welfare state. I wish only to emphasize the opportunity, since lost, which became available to forces concerned with the plight of the disadvantaged. What was a significant opening for progressive forces has become merely a rearguard action. The terrain will be left by default entirely to fiscal conservatives.

Endnotes

[1] Jane Jenson, "Representations in Crisis: The Roots of Canada's Permeable Fordism" (1990) XXXIII:4 Can. Journal of Political Science 653 at 664. Nancy Fraser has characterized this kind of contest as a "struggle over needs interpretation." See her *Unruly Practices: Power Discourse and Gender in Contemporary Social Theory* (Minneapolis: University of Minnesota Press, 1989) c.8.

[2] These social programs, particularly unemployment insurance, have not been saved from the federal government's cutbacks. See Robert M. Campbell, "Jobs...Job...Jo...J...The Conservatives and the Unemployed" in Frances Abele, ed., *How Ottawa Spends: The Politics of Competitiveness 1992-93* (Ottawa: Carleton University Press, 1992) at 32-35. Most recently, universal family allowances have been terminated.

[3] The following discussion borrows from *A Joint Venture: The Economics of Constitutional Options* (Ottawa: Supply and Services, 1991); Robin Boadway, *The Constitutional Division of Powers: An Economic Perspective* (A Study Prepared for the Economic Council of Canada) (Ottawa: Supply and Services, 1992); and Bradford Ried and Tracy Snodden, "Redistribution Under

Alternative Constitutional Arrangements for Canada" in Paul Boothe, ed., *Alberta and the Economics of Constitutional Change* (Edmonton: Western Centre for Economic Research, 1992).

4   For a discussion about "national standards" and their absence at present, see Lars Osberg, "The Economics of National Standards" (a research report prepared for the Government of Ontario: March 1992) ("'national standards' really are, at present, more myth than substance" at 59).

5   See C. Gray, "Medicare Under the Knife" *Saturday Night* (September 1991) at 11.

6   See "Abortion foes hope for victory in Saskatchewan" *The Globe & Mail* (6 May 1992) A1.

7   See discussion in Jim Silver, "Constitutional Change, Ideological Conflict and the Redistributive State" in James N. McCrorie and Martha L. MacDonald, eds, *The Constitutional Future of the Prairie and Atlantic Regions of Canada* (Regina: Canadian Plains Research Centre, 1992) 231 ff.

8   National Council of Welfare, *Funding Health and Higher Education: Danger Looming* (Ottawa: National Council of Welfare, Spring 1991) at 21.

9   National Council of Welfare, *The Canada Assistance Plan: No Time for Cuts* (Ottawa: National Council of Welfare, Winter 1991) at 3.

10 It generally is believed that it was Ontario's 1990-1991 budget which precipitated the federal government's constitutional proposal to co-ordinate fiscal and budgetary processes.

11 *Reference Re Canada Assistance Plan*, [1991] 6 W.W.R. 1 (S.C.C.).

12 Ontario, *Hansard* (27 March 1991) 276.

13 Ontario, *A Canadian Social Charter: Making Our Shared Values Stronger, A Discussion Paper* (Toronto: Ministry of Intergovernmental Affairs, September 1991) at 3.

14 *Ibid.* at 12-13.

15 *Ibid.* at 16.

16 *Ibid.* at 24.

17 S. Delacourt, "Ottawa to float concept of constitutional 'social charter'" *The Globe & Mail* (10 September 1991) A1.

18 The following discussion is drawn from David Schneiderman, "The Market and the Constitution" in D. Cameron and M. Smith, *Constitutional Politics* (Toronto: James Lorimer, 1991). The common market clause did not appear in the Charlottetown Accord but in a separate political accord to be discussed at a future First Ministers' Conference.

19 See Canada, *Powers Over the Economy: Securing the Canadian Economic Union in the Constitution* (Ottawa: Supply and Services, 1980).

20 See François Rocher, "Canadian Business and the Rhetoric of Economic Continentalization" (Summer 1991), 35 *Studies in Political Economy* 135-

154.

[21] For discussion regarding the volatility of business elite support for sovereignty see Édouard Cloutier, Jean H. Guay, and Daniel Latouche, *Le virage: l'Évolution de l'opinion publique au Québec depuis 1960* (Montréal: Québec/Amérique, 1992) at 130-140.

[22] Robin Boadway, *supra*, note 3 at 5.

[23] Economic Council of Canada, *supra*, note 3 at 67.

[24] See Kenneth Norrie, Robin Boadway, and Lars Osberg, "The Constitution and the Social Contract" in Robin W. Boadway, Thomas J. Courchene and Douglas D. Purvis, *Economic Dimensions of Constitutional Change*, vol. 1 (Kingston: John Deutsch Institute for the Study of Economic Policy, 1991) 225 at 242-244.

[25] I am grateful to Donna Greschner for having raised this point.

[26] "I suggest that the question of social protection, whether it is in the context of a social charter or some other means, must be part of our preoccupations" in "'Social Charter' Gathers Support," *The Globe & Mail* (1 February 1992) A1.

[27] "Canadians fear that increased economic efficiency will lead to the loss of 'the fundamental equity principles that bind us'" at *ibid*.

[28] *Ibid.*

[29] Antipoverty activists appeared to have been willing to engage in this trade-off. In the press release accompanying the antipoverty draft charter, there was no corresponding call to reject the conservative economic agenda included in the federal constitutional proposals.

[30] These and other issues are discussed in Jennifer Nedelsky and Craig Scott, "Constitutional Dialogue" (this volume).

[31] Robert W. Cox, "The Global Political Economy and Social Choice" in D. Drache and M.S. Gertler, *The New Era of Global Competition: State Policy and Market Power* (Montreal and Kingston: McGill-Queen's University Press, 1991).

[32] See Ramesh Mishra, *The Welfare State in Crisis: Social Thought and Social Change* (New York: St. Martin's Press, 1984) c.1.

[33] See Silver, *supra*, note 5 at 260. And see Gilles Breton and Jane Jenson, "After Free Trade and Meech Lake: Quoi de neuf?" (Spring 1991) 34 *Studies in Political Economy* 199 at 215.

10

Social Minima and Social Rights: Justifying Social Minima Socially

Glenn Drover

Introduction

National standards, according to some proponents of a social charter, are important to assure the high quality of service and benefit across Canada. Other proponents argue that national standards are essential simply to assure the ongoing commitment of the federal government to the social programs of the country. Still others state the case for standards on economic grounds. They claim that the developments resulting from free trade and international competition necessitate a labour force which is agile, mobile and able, as well as a population that is receptive to change. National commitments are important, they argue, to assure peace, order and (presumably) good investment, and to achieve change with a minimum amount of disruption, while protecting those who are most vulnerable. Finally, other proponents go beyond an argument of political commitment or economic advantage to suggest that national standards are inherent in the rights of citizenship.[1]

Regardless of the particular position that is taken, however, there is behind each argument a fundamental assumption that national standards, or (more generally) social minima, can be justified by appeals to principles of distributive justice. Yet when one turns to an examination of such principles, it is far from clear which social minima, and which national standards in particular, can be grounded in distributive justice. The reason for the ambiguity is that, while the basic concern underlying distributive justice and, presumably, national standards, is the fair share that each individual receives from the country in which she or he lives, and while political and moral philosophers agree that fairness should be grounded in equality, there is considerable debate about what constitutes equality.[2]

Depending on whether one favours equality of welfare, equality of respect, equality of resources, democratic equality, equality of opportunity, equal basic capabilities, or equal access to advantage, the case one makes for institutional arrangements will be different. In addition, depending upon the extent to which equality is or ought to be grounded in the linguistic and cultural communities with which one identifies (rather than in a nation state which is a federation of linguistic and cultural communities) or, alternatively, depending upon the extent to which personal elements and relationships of well-being (such as caring) are incorporated into social minima, national standards may or may not be appropriate in realizing the goal of equality. In order to see why this is the case, it is helpful to consider:

(1) the experience of Europe and Canada with respect to social minima;

(2) the debate about the difference between negative and positive rights;

(3) general egalitarianism;

(4) specific egalitarianism; and

(5) communitarian and feminist concerns with conventional arguments about distributive justice.

European and Canadian Experiences

Constitutional entrenchment of social minima within Europe has its roots in a conservative political tradition dating back to the last century. Guided by a principle of subsidiarity, constitutional guarantees are viewed as a way of balancing a respect for the family with the dignity of labour and the rights of private property. These guarantees are generally adopted within countries which have a strong tradition of Christian democracy or a long-standing association with the Catholic church.[3] Today, in most of the Constitutions of southern Europe as well as virtually all the countries of Latin and South America, a wide range of social minima related to state obligations is specified in constitutional law. European social charters are of more recent origin and have generally been fostered by progressive political forces as mechanisms for improving social programs. The European Social Charter is a counterpart to the European Convention on Human Rights which guarantees civil and political rights. A more recent charter, known as the Community Charter, is a product of the twelve countries which make up the European Economic Community. It focuses on the economic rights of workers. Unlike the more conservative tradition of constitutional protection, the social charters are treaties between member countries, specifying state obligations to move in an egalitarian direction, and are monitored by international committees which put external as well as internal pressure on countries to comply.

Furthermore, it is not just in constitutions and social charters that social minima are recognized. In countries where the Catholic church is not as strong as it is in southern Europe, or where egalitarian and social democratic principles are pervasive in political discourse, social minima are more likely to be specified in legislation than in constitutions. Examples of legislative standards are the social minimum of the Netherlands and the work councils of France. The social minimum of the Netherlands is a relative income concept which ties virtually all transfer payments, including social assistance, to the minimum wage. In a similar fashion, firms in France with 50 or more employees are required to establish councils if workers elect to do so. Where that decision is made, the firms are also obliged to pay up to 2% of the wage bill to cover the cost of social services for workers and their families. While the range of services varies from council to council, it includes programs such as social insurance, health care insurance, or even holiday resorts and camps.[4]

The social minima proposed in the Canadian Constitution have been frequently and incorrectly equated with the social charters of Europe. In reality, they are more in line with the European constitutional tradition in the sense that they are minimalist in the degree of their specificity and in the proposed means by which the obligations will be carried out. Nevertheless, since Canada has few legislated social minima, and virtually no national standards in terms of social programs other than in the area of health care, the inclusion of social goals in the Constitution, though largely symbolic, raises important questions about the merits of including social and economic rights in constitutional arrangements and about the distributive principles on which legislative minima such as those of Europe can be based. To understand those underlying principles and whether they can be used to justify social minima, I turn to a discussion about general egalitarianism and specific egalitarianism as justifications for distribution. Before doing so, I attempt to put to rest a false distinction which is often drawn between positive and negative rights.

The Debate around Positive and Negative Rights

There is a sharp debate about whether social and economic rights can really be recognized as rights in the same way as civil and political rights. Two criticisms which are often levelled against positive rights are that, unlike negative rights, they are not grounded in the intentionality of individual agents, and that they place potentially inexhaustible demands upon societal resources. Neither argument, however, seems to be founded on a solid moral or logical foundation.[5]

In rights discourse, there is broad agreement that negative or non-interference rights are a major way in which, in an open and democratic society, people demonstrate mutual respect for each other. For liberals like Hayek, negative rights are the only genuine expression of justice because they help to assure the autonomy of the person and are an indispensable link between justice and individual freedom. Central to Hayek's thesis is the idea that justice is about universal rules which assure individual autonomy, not about balancing social interests. Hence, injustice arises from the intentional acts of individuals or groups who interfere in the freedom of others, and societies which are guided by just and universalizable rules cannot be classified as unjust simply because it is individuals, not societies, who have intentionality. In a free and open market, therefore, those who end up being poor or at risk of being poor because of the workings of the market cannot claim that they have been unjustly treated, only that they have been unfortunate in the lottery of life. The Hayekian view of justice is that individual rights and freedoms must prevail and any attempt to use the state to accomplish some predetermined end, no matter how noble, in the name of distributive justice, will lead to injustice.[6]

To appreciate the limitations of Hayek's defence of negative rights and his attack on positive rights, it is important to assess the argument about the unintended nature of market allocations. Setting aside the lack of attention to historical determinants of existing market allocations which Hayek generally ignores, and even acknowledging that we cannot predict the outcome of market transactions for individuals, it is untrue (as Raymond Plant points out) that one cannot make a judgement about the effect of market allocations on groups.[7] Since opponents of positive rights, like Hayek, know that as a matter of routine the intended actions of individuals in the market produce a foreseeable but unintended outcome for another person, it is disingenuous for them to claim that they cannot assume some responsibility for the foreseeable but unintended consequences of their actions. Justice is not only a question of the intention of the action, or the genesis of a particular problem, but also about the response to a particular outcome. Aside from the presumed lack of intentionality inherent in market transactions, and the implicit illegitimacy of claims based on distributive justice, another criticism usually levelled against the notion of positive rights is that, unlike negative rights, the cost implications are open-ended. The accusation has frequently been heard from those who oppose the inclusion of social goals or rights in the revision of the Canadian Constitution. The high cost of social rights, it is claimed, establish two essential restrictions. The first is simply that a claim is necessarily limited since it is made against scarce resources and must be ranked against other such claims, and ranking implies at best that positive rights are partial rights, since they can never be fully realized even in the most affluent society. The second restriction flows from the first, in the sense that, since the realization of positive rights depends upon affluence, they can never be universal in the manner of negative rights because poor countries do not have the capacity to deliver.

In response to these criticisms, it must first be pointed out that the protection of negative rights is far from cost-free. More importantly, as the recent riots in Los Angeles and Toronto have shown, the duty of forbearance is not likely to be highly respected unless people have access to some of the resources implicit in positive rights claims. While the costs of negative rights might be quite limited in a world of saints, the fact is that in the everyday world of sinners people need a sense of solidarity with others based upon some commonly perceived egalitarian principles. In general, therefore, there is little principled difference in the implications for scarcity of positive and negative rights because, while the former imply limited material resources, the latter imply limited motivational resources. Secondly, with respect to the criticism about affluence, it is important to recognize that claims to positive rights are based on role expectations which will necessarily vary from society to society. The universal nature of a positive rights claim need not be based on the availability of equal amounts of resources beyond a basic minimum, but tied instead to a desirable outcome.

General Egalitarianism

Challenging the distinction which is often drawn between positive and negative rights may give grounds for asserting the potential for social minima, but it does not say much about the rationality of a positive rights claim or the extent to which social minima should be asserted. The first issue (the rationality of positive rights) is addressed by general egalitarianism, the second (the extent of minima) by specific egalitarianism. According to Albert Weale, the rationality of a positive rights claim is based on a principle of autonomy within a system of social choice, which implies a prescription for minimum standards of institutional provision.[8] The argument for autonomy is in turn based upon an assumption of universalizability. In ranking or ordering collective intervention in the lives of people, the first priority must be given to autonomy because it is only through human freedom and reflexivity that personal projects can be realized, and that individuals can regulate their conduct within a public set of principles which are broadly and voluntarily accepted. For persons to be capable of autonomous action, however, two conditions are needed: the freedom to act without interference and the absence of deprivation. Without either of these conditions being met, the chances for autonomous rational action are severely limited. Two authors who have interpreted equal liberty in these terms are John Rawls and Ronald Dworkin. While there are significant differences between the two, they share an assumption that natural endowments (i.e., personal capabilities) are, from a moral perspective, arbitrary and therefore the benefits of these endowments are to be treated as collective assets.

Rawls' principles of justice are well known and need little elaboration here. His central idea is that all primary goods such as liberty and opportunities, income and wealth, self-respect and powers are to be distributed equally, unless an unequal distribution is to the benefit of the least advantaged, and on the condition that offices and positions are open to all on the basis of equal opportunity. The distinctive feature of primary goods is that they are essential if all individuals are to accomplish the projects or attain the ways of life they think appropriate. Thus Rawls treats people as equals by removing only those inequalities, namely income and wealth, which disadvantage someone. But inequalities are allowed if it can be shown that they lead to improvements for the least disadvantaged over time. The case for Rawlsian distributive justice is based on two arguments: limitations on the principle of equal opportunity and a social contract made behind a veil of ignorance.[9] Rawls does not disagree with the principle of equal opportunity, but considers that it does not go far enough. While it recognizes injustices derived from social circumstance and legitimizes the need for nondiscrimination in employment or even affirmative action, it ignores inequalities in natural talents. The rewards of both social circumstance and natural talents need to be qualified by their contribution to those with the fewest advantages. As for his social contract argument, the main purpose of it is to demonstrate that equality of primary goods is a rational outcome of discussion and debate, if the participants were organizing a society without knowing in advance the advantages or disadvantages, in social and natural circumstances, that each would have.

The problem with Rawls' theory, as Kymlicka and others have shown, is that it makes too many assumptions about human nature.[10] One questionable assumption is that all people behind a veil of ignorance are naturally sympathetic to those who are most disadvantaged, and adjust their expectations of primary goods accordingly. If, instead of playing it safe, the participants have a greater propensity to take risks, they may be willing to opt for less than an equal distribution of primary goods on the ground that they stand to gain more if they are not among the most disadvantaged. Another criticism is that Rawls places emphasis on the original distribution of natural endowments, not on the choices people make with the endowments they have.

Ronald Dworkin, in his theory of equal resources, attempts to compensate for Rawls' inadequacies by developing a case for egalitarianism that is "ambition-sensitive" and "endowment-insensitive."[11] The core of Dworkin's theory is the distinction he draws between an individual's personality and personal circumstances. The definition of personality includes convictions, ambitions, tastes and preferences. The definition of circumstances includes talents, skills and capacities, both physical and mental. For Dworkin what counts is the distributional equality of circumstances. People are considered to be equal in their circumstances when resources are distributed so as to allow for differentials in unequal talent and capacities, or (as Jacobs puts it) when the cost of one person to others is equal to the cost of everyone else. Since, however, people will choose to do different things with their circumstances depending upon their personalities, some will come to have control over more resources than others. However, for Dworkin, this does not mean they do not have equal resources, provided that the differentials in talents and capacities are taken into account over the lifetime of the individual.

The essential problem with general egalitarianism, however, both of the Rawlsian and Dworkinian type, is that, while it provides a rationale for the establishment of social minima, it is vague about the level or extent of the minima and the institutions which are necessary to realize individual autonomy. Weale seems to suggest that general egalitarianism implies not only a minimum level of income to offset poverty, and a level of education to allow people to deliberate and plan for the options and choices which are available to them, but also minimal distribution of private property in order to decentralize decision making. With respect to income, he also proposes that minimum standards be nationwide to avoid large differentials or arbitrary treatment of citizens in the same country.[12] He states that there should be minima in each of these areas; however, he is less sanguine about an appeal to autonomy as a basis for distributive justice and concludes that more precise standards require consideration of specific egalitarianism. Kymlicka, too, is uncertain about the implications of general egalitarianism. On the one hand, he implies that the theories of Rawls and Dworkin are consistent with minimalist state interventions. On the other hand, he suggests that these theories have more radical implications than their authors acknowledge or wish to accept, although exactly what these implications are he does not disclose.[13]

Specific Egalitarianism

A major difference between general and specific egalitarianism is that while the former relies upon a concept of right which is neutral with regard to the good, the latter uses the concept of need to postulate some fundamentals of the good. While one hypothesizes a general minimum as a basis of autonomy, the other prescribes the nature of the minimum as a standard of well-being. In short, specific egalitarianism not only states that a certain degree of equality is essential for the good life, but that a more equal distribution is ethically preferable to a less equal distribution, although precisely what that distribution should be remains (and likely will remain) contestable. In social policy parlance, it goes beyond in-cash transfers to deal with in-kind or targeted transfers.

Two recent theories which have argued the case for specific minima are grounded in a theory of need. Braybrooke states that in every society there are certain course-of-life needs which are universal and essential if human beings are to live and function. Each of these needs, he asserts, can be defined within a given linguistic community by minimum standards of provision, a criterion for inclusion, and a principle of precedence. With regard to minimum standards, he seems to suggest that experts can make a decision of fact on a standard (as in the case of food) around an average, while taking into account individual and cultural variation. Regarding a criterion of inclusion, he discusses the importance of basic social roles, particularly the roles of parent, householder, worker, and citizen. As to the principle of precedence, he implies that once a reference population and a standard of fact have been identified, the need so circumscribed takes priority over personal preferences and the resources of the society. The idea behind this approach is to remove the discussion of needs (as distinct from wants) away from relativistic notions based on political prescription and to link need with harm or ailing.[14]

Doyal and Gough take these insights further and claim that the satisfaction of universalizable needs for physical health and autonomy require universal preconditions which enable minimally impaired participation in the forms of life in which people find themselves. The preconditions for meeting needs, which follow very closely the basic social roles identified by Braybrooke, are production, reproduction, cultural transmission, and authority. The right to minimal need satisfaction (i.e., negative rights) is grounded in the nature of human agency as a bearer of responsibility, and in correlative duty, which is common to all cultures. If this is accepted, the ascription of duty implies a belief that the bearer is entitled to a level of need satisfaction necessary for her to meet her obligations. The right to optimal need satisfaction (i.e., positive rights) is based on the idea that a commitment to the conception of shared goods which is peculiar to a given culture presupposes a reasonable distribution of the available resources in that culture to make the attainment of the shared good a realistic possibility. The intermediate needs which are required to satisfy the basic needs of physical health and autonomy are: food and water, protective housing, a nonhazardous work environment, appropriate health care, security in childhood, physical security, economic security, appropriate education, and safe birth control and child-bearing. These are examined at the level of the nation-state which is taken to be the arbiter of social minima.[15]

Communitarian and Feminist Concerns

What is obvious from an examination of Doyal and Gough is the extension of the defence of social minima from considerations of income and wealth to considerations of health and education, from general to specific egalitarianism, and from in-cash to in-kind distribution. What is less obvious is whether they have escaped or can escape a charge of cultural relativism and why, since they have developed no theory of citizenship rights, they have used the nation state as the basis for cultural standards. According to communitarians, it is not only unwise but impossible to attempt to escape cultural relativism. For this reason, they reject the arguments of general egalitarianism associated with Rawls and Dworkin, not only because of the assumed neutrality of the state inherent in their approach but also because communitarians, like specific egalitarians, support a politic of the common good. Unlike the latter, however, communitarians would appear to be less inclined to argue the case for such universal minima as some quantifiable standard of need, because it is only through given cultures that people can determine and specify meaningful options. Social minima or standards, therefore, are bound to be culturally structured. As Walzer sees it, need claims in specific cases embody understandings which, though widely shared, are determined within a particular community. Any attempt to stipulate those needs philosophically or professionally removes them from the political realm where they rightfully belong.[16] Nancy Fraser puts the same thesis somewhat bluntly when she states that beyond a very thin notion of needs, all thick notions are eminently contestable.[17]

Aside from the critique of the foundational claims of general and specific egalitarianism, what is perhaps more to the point about communitarianism is the implication that social minima are grounded at best and by preference in the ways of life of particular communities, and while these communities may coincide with the nation-state, they need not necessarily be so. In fact, language or race or ethnicity, as is increasingly evident throughout the world as well as in Canada, are just as often, and sometimes more often, the defining characteristic of community rather than the nation-state. The fundamental reason for this is that our very notions of rights and needs are linguistic concepts and cultural practices which form a part of everyday practice and can only be understood in this context. What is conceived as good, particularly a common good, therefore, is more likely to be linguistically or culturally conditioned than politically determined. To the extent that social minima express these shared understandings, they secure community. To the extent that they do not, they may even be a potential affront to the distributive justice they are intended to interpret. The nation state may not be the best guarantor of those values which linguistic and cultural communities cherish the most.

Two other concerns about general and specific egalitarianism which bear upon the appropriateness of social minima have been raised by feminists. They are the inattention, in theories of distributive justice, to distinctions between the private and the public and between justice and care. One of the more pressing concerns about the former distinction is that while the public has usually been associated with adult males, the private or domestic life has been treated as almost exclusively a female responsibility. Thus, when theories of justice are discussed, rights, and social rights in particular, have tended to be defined in gender terms (i.e., with respect to their effect on public relations rather than private relations and with little regard to the protection of domestic relations). Hence, women's personal autonomy has usually been confounded with family autonomy.[18]

Another consequence of the public-private distinction is that men and women tend to reason in different voices, with men focusing on competing rights and obligations, and women focusing on relationships and caring. And while the two may not be incompatible, there can be little doubt that the implications of caring have received less attention than have rights, in public discourse and in theories of distributive justice. Furthermore, as Tronto points out, an ethic of caring contrasts development of moral dispositions (caring) with an understanding of moral principles (justice), particularity of response (caring) with universal applicability (justice), and attending to relationships (caring) with attending to rights and fairness (justice).[19] The essential question which the distinctions raise is how an ethic of caring thus defined fits into social minima or national standards. The answer has to be: not easily. Yet, as many feminists would argue, unless caring is configured into public expressions of distributive justice, women's concern with subjectively experienced hurt will likely be subordinate to men's concern for objective unfairness. It may be impossible, as Kymlicka suggests, to incorporate an ethic of caring into an ethic of justice, except implicitly, in the sense that a recognition of rights or needs or both is reciprocated by an obligation for caring responsibilities. However, another significant problem, as Kymlicka also allows, is that the distribution of care remains an issue of justice which has too long been associated with a female, and frequently unpaid, proletariat.[20] Unless this is publicly taken into account, the advantages of justice, including their legislated or constitutional expression in social minima, will likely continue to be interpreted in a manly direction.

Conclusion

Can social minima be justified socially? If one is persuaded that survival and equal autonomy are foundational to human agency, it is difficult to answer in any other way than by saying yes. Both principles assert that all persons everywhere are entitled to a basic minimum, within the resources available to a society, allowing them to live with dignity and respect, and that governments have an obligation to ensure that conditions exist by which survival and equal autonomy are possible. This obligation is not the same as the responsibility of government to maximize the welfare of every individual, but only the responsibility to create the conditions possible for the latter to come about. Even this minimalist argument, however, can be used to make a case, based on need, that governments have some obligation to ensure in-kind transfers as well as in-cash transfers when survival is interpreted to mean (as surely it must) a modicum of physical and mental health, and autonomy to incorporate participation and critical reflection. On the other hand, if there is also some validity to the concerns of the communitarians, social minima do not imply, in a federal state like Canada, the necessity for national standards. This is especially so if those standards override, or are perceived to override, the legitimate aspirations of linguistic and cultural minorities. Equally, if the criticisms of distributive justice by feminists are taken into account, it is even possible that social minima as they now stand will not only help to reinforce gender bias and patriarchy but also understate the element of care which is essential to the realization of justice.

Endnotes

[1] These different perspectives are expressed in varying degrees by Terry Hunsley, "Constitutional Change and Social Programs," in *The State of the Nation* (Kingston: Queens University, Institute for Intergovernmental Relations, 1991); Lars Osberg, *The Economics of National Standards* (Halifax: Dalhousie University, 1991); Institute of Intergovernmental Relations, *Approaches to National Standards in Federal Systems* (Kingston: Institute of Intergovernmental Relations, 1991); Ontario Ministry of the Attorney General, *The Protection of Social and Economic Rights: A Comparative Study* (Toronto: Ministry of the Attorney General, 1991); Echenberg et al, *A Social Charter for Canada* (Toronto: C.D. Howe Institute, 1992); Social Planning Council of Metropolitan Toronto, "The Social Policy Implications of the Constitution" (1992) 11:4 *Social Infopac*.

[2]   The literature on equality is extensive. I note only a few volumes. One of the most well known early texts is by R. H. Tawney, *Equality* (London: Allen and Unwin, 1931), but Tawney's attack on inequality left no consensus of its opposite. A more recent text, somewhat in the same tradition, is by Albert Weale, *Equality and Social Policy* (London: Routledge and Kegan Paul, 1978). For philosophical articles, see Ronald Dworkin, "What is Equality?" (Parts 1 and 2) (1981) *Philosophy and Public Affairs* 185-246 and 283-345.

[3]   An excellent summary of the different traditions of social policy associated with social and Christian democracy can be found in Kees van Kersbergen, *Social Capitalism: A Study of Christian Democracy and the Post War Settlement of the Welfare State* (Florence: European University Institute, 1991).

[4]   For a discussion of legislative approaches, see Pat Kerans, Glenn Drover, and David Williams, *Welfare and Worker Participation* (Basingstoke: MacMillan, 1988).

[5]   I draw upon Raymond Plant for these distinctions and the discussion which follows. See Raymond Plant, *Modern Political Thought* (N.P.: Basil Blackwell, 1991); also R. Plant, H. Lesser, and P. Taylor-Gooby, *Political Philosophy and Social Welfare* (London: Routledge and Kegan Paul, 1981).

[6]   Hayek develops these ideas, here and there, in several of his texts, but see in particular, *Law Legislation and Liberty Vol 2: The Mirage of Social Justice* (Chicago: University of Chicago Press, 1976) 60-75, and *The Constitution of Liberty* (Chicago: University of Chicago Press, 1960).

[7]   Plant, *Modern Political Thought*, *supra*, note 5 at 265-291.

[8]   Albert Weale, *Political Theory and Social Policy* (London: Macmillan, 1983) at 7.

[9]   John Rawls, *A Theory of Justice* (Oxford: Oxford University Press, 1972) and "The Basic Liberties and Their Priority" in Sterling M. McMurrin, *Liberty Equality and Law* (Salt Lake City: University of Utah Press, 1987).

[10] Will Kymlicka, *Contemporary Political Philosophy* (Oxford: Clarendon Press, 1990) and *Liberalism Community and Culture* (Oxford: Clarendon Press, 1989).

[11] Ronald Dworkin, "What Is Equality? Part 2, Equality of Resources" (1981) 10 *Philosophy and Public Affairs* at 283-345; "In Defence of Equality" (1983) 1:1 *Social Philosophy and Policy*. I draw upon a summary of Dworkin's ideas in Lesley Jacobs, *Equal Life Prospects: A Perfectionist Theory of Fair Shares* (Paper presented at the Canadian Political Science Association Annual Meetings, 1992).

[12] Weale, *Political Theory and Social Policy*, *supra*, note 8, c.3 and 6.

[13] Kymlicka, *Contemporary Political Philosophy*, *supra*, note 10.

[14] David Braybrooke, *Meeting Needs* (Princeton: Princeton University Press, 1987); see in particular c.2.

[15] Len Doyal, and Ian Gough, *A Theory of Human Need* (Basingstoke: MacMillan Education, 1991). Doyal and Gough develop a philosophical rationale for the universalizability of need as a basis of social intervention and link it with the political economy of need determination.

[16] Michael Walzer, *Spheres of Justice* (New York: Basic Books, 1983).

[17] Nancy Fraser, *Unruly Practices: Power, Discourse and Gender in Contemporary Social Theory* (Minneapolis: University of Minnesota Press, 1989).

[18] R.W. Connell, *Gender and Power: Society, The Person and Sexual Politics* (Stanford: Stanford University Press, 1987).

[19] J. Tronto, "Beyond Gender Difference to a Theory of Care" (1987) 12 *Signs* 644.

[20] Kymlicka, *Contemporary Political Philosophy, supra,* note 10. The philosophical literature on communitarianism and feminism is neatly summarized by Kymlicka. I draw upon his summary but I do not agree with his conclusions.

Appendix I
Draft Social Charter*

Part 1

Social and Economic Rights

1. In light of Canada's international and domestic commitments to respect, protect and promote the human rights of all members of Canadian society, and, in particular, members of its most vulnerable and disadvantaged groups, everyone has an equal right to well-being, including a right to:
   (a) a standard of living that ensures adequate food, clothing, housing, child care, support services and other requirements for security and dignity of the person and for full social and economic participation in their communities and in Canadian society;
   (b) health care that is comprehensive, universal, portable, accessible, and publicly administered, including community-based non-profit delivery of services;

---

* As released March 27, 1992 from the National Anti-Poverty Organization by a broad coalition of concerned citizens, organizations and constitutional experts from St. John's to Vancouver.

    (c) public primary and secondary education, accessible post-secondary and vocational education, and publicly-funded education for those with special needs arising from disabilities;

    (d) access to employment opportunities; and

    (e) just and favourable conditions of work, including the right of workers to organize and bargain collectively.

2.   The Canadian Charter of Rights and Freedoms shall be interpreted in a manner consistent with the rights in s.1 and the fundamental value of alleviating and eliminating social and economic disadvantage.

3.   Nothing contained in s.1 diminishes or limits the rights contained in the Canadian Charter of Rights and Freedoms.

4.   Governments have obligations to improve the conditions of life of children and youth and to take positive measures to ameliorate the historical and social disadvantage of groups facing discrimination.

5.   Statutes, regulations, policy, practice and the common law shall be interpreted and applied in a manner consistent with the rights in s.1 and the fundamental value of alleviating and eliminating social and economic disadvantage.

6.   Any legislation and federal-provincial agreements related to fulfilment of the rights in section 1 through national shared cost programs shall have the force of law, shall not be altered except in accordance with their terms and shall be enforceable at the instance of any party or of any person adversely affected upon application to a court of competent jurisdiction.

7.   (1) The federal government has a special role and responsibility to fund federal-provincial shared cost programs with a view to the achievement of a comparable level and quality of services throughout the federation, in accordance with s.36.

      (2) Accordingly, federal funding shall reflect the relative cost and capacity of delivering such programs in the various provinces, with equalization payments where required to address serious disparities in relative cost and capacity.

(3) The federal government and provincial governments shall conduct taxation and other fiscal policies in a manner consistent with these responsibilities and with their obligations under shared cost programs.

8. The provisions of sections 1 to 7 shall apply to territorial governments where appropriate.

Part II

Social Rights Council

9. (1) By [a specified date], there shall be established by the [REFORMED] Senate of Canada the Social Rights Council (the Council) to evaluate the extent to which federal and provincial law and practice is in compliance with the rights contained in s.1.

   (2) In evaluating compliance the Council shall:

   (a) establish and revise standards according to which compliance with the rights in s.1 can be evaluated;

   (b) compile information and statistics on the social and economic circumstances of individuals with respect to the rights in s.1, especially those who are members of vulnerable and disadvantaged groups;

   (c) assess the level of compliance of federal and provincial law and practice with respect to the rights in s.1;

   (d) educate the public and appropriate government officials;

   (e) submit recommendations to appropriate governments and legislative bodies;

   (f) encourage governments to engage in active and meaningful consultations with non-governmental organizations which are representative of vulnerable and disadvantaged members of society; and

   (g) carry out any other task that is necessary or appropriate for the purpose.

(3) In evaluating compliance with Part I the Council shall have the power to:

   (a) hold inquiries and require attendance by individuals, groups or appropriate government officials;

   (b) require that necessary and relevant information, including documents, reports and other materials, be provided by governments; and

   (c) require any government to report on matters relevant to compliance.

(4) The government or legislative body to which recommendations in s.9(2)(e) are addressed has an obligation to respond in writing to the Council within three months.

(5) With respect to Canada's obligations under international reporting procedures that relate to the rights in s.1, the Council shall:

   (a) assist in the preparation of Canada's reports under such procedures;

   (b) actively consult with non-governmental organizations representative of vulnerable and disadvantaged groups, and encourage governments to engage in similar consultations;

   (c) have the right to append separate opinions to the final versions of such reports before or after they are submitted to the appropriate international body; and

   (d) make available a representative of the Council to provide any information requested by the appropriate international body.

(6) The Council shall respond to any request for information or invitation to intervene from the Tribunal established under s.10 and the Council shall have the right to intervene in any proceedings before the Tribunal.

(7) The Council shall be independent and shall be guaranteed public funding through Parliament sufficient for it to carry out its functions.

(8) Persons appointed to the Council shall have demonstrated experience in the area of social and economic rights and a commitment to the objectives of the Social Charter.

(9) (a) All appointments to the Council shall be made by the [REFORMED] Senate of Canada.

  (b) One-third of the appointments shall be from nominations from each of the following sectors:

    (i) the federal government;

    (ii) provincial and territorial governments; and

    (iii) non-governmental organizations representing vulnerable and disadvantaged groups.

 (10) [self-governing aboriginal communities]

Part III

Social Rights Tribunal

10. (1) By [a specified date], there shall be established by the [REFORMED] Senate of Canada the Social Rights Tribunal of the Federation (the Tribunal) which shall receive and consider petitions from individuals and groups alleging infringements of rights under s.1.

 (2) The Tribunal shall have as its main purpose the consideration of selected petitions alleging infringements that are systemic or that have significant impact on vulnerable or disadvantaged groups and their members.

 (3) The Tribunal shall have the power to consider and review federal and provincial legislation, regulations, programs, policies or practices, including obligations under federal-provincial agreements.

 (4) Where warranted by the purpose set out in s.10(2), the Tribunal shall:

  (a) hold hearings into allegations of infringements of any right under s.1; and

  (b) issue decisions as to whether a right has been infringed.

 (5) Where the Tribunal decides that a right has been infringed it shall:

  (a) hear submission from petitioners and governments as to measures that are required to achieve compliance with the rights in s.1 and as to time required to carry out such measures; and

(b) order that measures be taken by the appropriate government within a specified period of time.

(6) (a) In lieu of issuing an order under s.10(5)(b), the Tribunal shall, where appropriate, order that the appropriate government report back by a specified date on measures taken or proposed to be taken which will achieve compliance with the rights in s.1.

(b) Upon receiving a report under s.10(6)(a), the Tribunal may issue another order under s.10(6)(a) or issue an order under s.19(5)(b).

(7) (a) An order of the Tribunal for measures under s.10(5)(b) shall not come into effect until the House of Commons or the relevant legislature has sat for at least five weeks, during which time the decision may be overridden by a simple majority vote of that legislature or Parliament.

(b) The relevant government may indicate its acceptance of the terms of an order of the Tribunal under s.10(5)(b) prior to the expiry of the period specified in s.10(6)(a).

(8) Tribunal decisions and orders shall be subject to judicial review only the Supreme Court of Canada and only for manifest error of jurisdiction.

(9) The Tribunal may, at any stage, request information from, request investigation by, or invite the intervention of the Social Rights Council.

(10) The Tribunal shall be made accessible to members of disadvantaged groups and their representative organizations by all reasonable means, including the provision of necessary funding by appropriate governments.

(11) The Tribunal shall be independent and shall be guaranteed public funding through Parliament sufficient for it to carry out its functions.

(12) (a) All appointments to the Tribunal shall be made by the [REFORMED] Senate of Canada.

(b) One-third of the appointments shall be from each of the following sectors:

(i) the federal government;

(ii) provincial and territorial governments; and

(iii) non-governmental organizations representing vulnerable and disadvantaged groups.

(13) [The Province of Quebec] [Any province] may exclude the competence of the Tribunal with respect to matters within its jurisdiction by establishing a comparable tribunal or conferring competence on an existing tribunal.

(14) [self-governing aboriginal communities]

Part IV

Environmental Rights

11. In view of the fundamental importance of the natural environment and the necessity for ecological integrity,
   (a) everyone has a right:
      (i) to a healthful environment;
      (ii) to redress and remedy for those who have suffered or will suffer environmental harm;* and
      (iii) to participate in decision making with respect to activities likely to have a significant effect on the environment;
   (b) all government are trustees of public lands, waters and resources for present and future generations.

---

* A Note on Enforcement of Environmental Rights: The Canadian Environmental Law Association, Pollution Probe, and the Constitutional Caucus of the Canadian Environmental Network endorse an amendment to the Canadian Charter of Rights and Freedoms protecting the right to a healthy environment.

This is not to say that the mechanism for enforcement of environmental rights must rely solely on the courts. The proposed Environmental Bill of Rights for Ontario provides an example of an enforcement mechanism by a specialized tribunal.

Appendix II
Ontario's Proposal for a
Social Charter for Canada*

I.   Entrenching the Principles

(1) The social charter should constitutionally entrench the positive obligations of governments to provide social programs and set national standards. Ontario proposes that the social charter be entrenched in section 36 of the *Constitution Act, 1982,* and that it speak in terms of the commitment of governments to meet social policy objectives.

(2) A limited expression of social principles is already included in the Canadian Constitution. Section 36(1) of the *Constitution Act, 1982,* currently reads:

36(1) Without altering the legislative authority of Parliament or of the provincial legislatures, or the rights of any of them with respect to the exercise of their legislative authority, Parliament and the legislatures, together with the government of Canada and the provincial governments are committed to

(a) promoting equal opportunities for the well-being of Canadians;

---

* As released, February 13, 1992 from the Office of the Premier Bob Rae.

(b) furthering economic development to reduce disparity in opportunities; and

(c) providing essential public services of reasonable quality to all Canadians.

Ontario proposes that the following principles be added to section 36(1):

(d) providing throughout Canada a health care program that is comprehensive, universal, portable, publicly administered, and accessible;

(e) providing social services and welfare based on need, so as to ensure that all Canadians have access to a minimum level of housing, food, and other basic necessities;

(f) providing high quality public primary and secondary education to all persons resident in Canada;

(g) protecting, preserving and improving the quality of the environment within a sustainable economy, and

(h) generally promoting the quality and standard of life of Canadians.

(3) The benefits of our social programs should be available to Canadians as they move to take residence in different provinces. Ontario proposes that section 6 of the *Canadian Charter of Rights and Freedoms* be amended to expand the current definition of mobility rights with respect to social benefits.

(4) Entrenching the social obligations of governments in the Constitution must not weaken the rights currently enjoyed by Canadians. Ontario proposes that a clause be included in the social charter to ensure that it operates in harmony with the *Canadian Charter of Rights and Freedoms*.

II. Implementation and Monitoring

(5) An important element of the social charter is the commitment of governments to cooperate in funding social programs. Ontario proposes that agreements reach by governments in the areas covered by the social charter should be made constitutionally binding.

(6) Governments must be held accountable for the decisions they take or fail to take, in relation to the social charter. These actions, therefore, should be monitored by an independent and open mechanism. This mechanism could be established either in a reformed Senate or as an independent body. Ontario proposes that an independent commission be established to monitor the implementation of the social charter. The Commission will:

- be appointed jointly by Canada and the provinces;
- report annually on governments' progress in meeting social charter commitments, including the implementation of intergovernmental agreements;
- conduct public hearings on matters related to the social charter and examine questions related to the failure of governments to meet their social charter obligations;
- make recommendations to governments in relation to their social charger commitments; and
- establish expert panels to engage in research on specific social policy issues.

(7) National standards are very important to Canadians. At present, it is sometimes difficult to develop national standards because intergovernmental decision-making often requires unanimity. Ontario proposes that intergovernmental decision-making be made less restrictive, in order to allow for the development and harmonization of standards as soon as the majority of the provinces agree.

Appendix III

Report of the Special Joint Committee on a Renewed Canada (Beaudoin-Dobbie)*

The Social Covenant and the Economic Union

The title to Part III of the *Constitution Act, 1982* would be amended to read "THE SOCIAL COVENANT AND THE ECONOMIC UNION" and the following sections would be added to Part III:

Social Covenant

36.1 (1) Parliament, the legislatures and the territorial councils, together with the government of Canada and the provincial and territorial governments, are jointly committed to

(a) providing throughout Canada a health care system that is comprehensive, universal, portable, publicly administered, and accessible;

---

3 From *A Renewed Canada – The Report of the Special Joint Committee on a Renewed Canada*, Joint Chairmen: Hon. Gérald Beaudoin, Senator and Dorothy Dobbie, M.P., February 28, 1992, Third Session of the Thirty-fourth Parliament, 1991-92.

(b) providing adequate social services and benefits to ensure that all Canadians have reasonable access to housing, food and other basic necessities;

(c) providing high quality public primary and secondary education to all persons resident in Canada and ensuring reasonable access to post-secondary education;

(d) protecting the rights of workers to organize and bargain collectively, and

(e) protecting and preserving the integrity of the environment in an economically sustainable manner.

Review Agency

(2) The *[intergovernmental agency to be established]* shall review, assess and report on the performance of the federal, provincial and territorial governments in meeting the goals of the Social Covenant stated in subsection (1).

Economic Union

36.2 (1) Parliament, the legislatures and the territorial councils, together with the government of Canada and the provincial and territorial governments are jointly committed to

(a) working together to strengthen the Canadian economic union;

(b) free movement of persons, goods, services and capital; and

(c) the goal of full employment; and

(d) ensuring that all Canadians have a reasonable standard of living.

Review Agency

(2) The *[intergovernmental agency to be established]* shall review, assess and report on the performance of the federal, provincial and territorial governments in meeting the goals of the Economic Union stated in subsection (1).

Tabling of Reports

36.3 The reports of the *[agency]* under subsection 36.1(2) or 36.2(2) shall be laid before Parliament, the legislatures of the provinces and the councils of the territories.

Legislative Authority Not Altered

36.4 Sections 36.1 to 36.3 do not alter the legislative authority of Parliament, the provincial legislatures or the territorial councils, or the rights of any of them with respect to the exercise of their legislative authority.

Appendix IV

Consensus Report on the Constitution – Charlottetown Final Text*

Canada's Social and Economic Union

4. *The Social and Economic Union*

A new provision should be added to the Constitution describing the commitment of the governments, Parliament and the legislatures within the federation to the principle of the preservation and development of Canada's social and economic union. The new provision, entitled *The Social and Economic Union*, should be drafted to set out a series of policy objectives underlying the social and the economic union, respectively. The provision should not be justiciable.

The policy objectives set out in the provision on the social union should include, but not be limited to:
* providing throughout Canada a health care system that is comprehensive, universal, portable, publicly administered and accessible;

*   As released, August 28, 1992.

- providing adequate social services and benefits to ensure that all individuals resident in Canada have reasonable access to housing, food and other basic necessities;
- providing high quality primary and secondary education to all individuals resident in Canada and ensuring reasonable access to post-secondary education;
- protecting the rights of workers to organize and bargain collectively; and,
- protecting, preserving and sustaining the integrity of the environment for present and future generations.

The policy objectives set out in the provision on the economic union should include, but not be limited to:

- working together to stregthen the Canadian economic union;
- the free movement of persons, goods, services and capital;
- the goal of full employment;
- ensuring that all Canadians have a reasonable standard of living; and,
- ensuring sustainable and equitable development.

A mechanism for monitoring the Social and Economic Union should be determined by a First Ministers' Conference.

A clause should be added to the Constitution stating that the Social and Economic Union does not abrogate or derogate from the *Canadian Charter of Rights and Freedoms*.

5. *Economic Disparities, Equalization and Regional Development*

Section 36 of the *Constitution Act, 1982* currently commits Parliament and the Government of Canada and the governments and legislatures of the provinces to promote equal opportunities and economic development throughout the country and to provide reasonably comparable levels of public services to all Canadians. Subsection 36(2) currently commits the federal government to the principle of equalization payments. This section should be amended to read as follows:

Parliament and the Government of Canada are committed to making equalization payments so that provincial governments have sufficient revenues to provide reasonably comparable levels of public services at reasonably comparable levels of taxation.

Subsection 36(1) should be expanded to include the territories.

Subsection 36(1) should be amended to add a commitment to ensure the provision of reasonably comparable economic infrastructures of a national nature in each province and territory.

The Constitution should commit the federal government to meaningful consultation with the provinces before introducing legislation relating to equalization payments.

A new Subsection 36(3) should be added to entrench the commitment of governments to the promotion of regional economic development to reduce economic disparities.

Regional development is also discussed in item 36 of this document.

6. *The Common Market*

Section 121 of the *Constitution Act, 1867* would remain unchanged.

Detailed principles and commitments related the Canadian Common Market are included in the political accord of August 28, 1992. First Ministers will decide on the best approach to implement these principles and commitments at a future First Ministers' Conference on the economy. First Ministers would have the authority to create an independent dispute resolution agency and decide on its role, mandate and composition. (*)

Appendix V

Charlottetown Accord Draft Legal Text*

The Social and Economic Union

36.1 (1) Without altering the authority of Parliament, the provincial legislatures or the territorial legislative authorities,
or of the government of Canada or the governments of
the provinces or territories, or the rights of any of them
with respect to the exercise of their authority, Parliament,
the provincial legislatures and the territorial legislative
authorities, together with the government of Canada and
the provincial and territorial government, are committed
to the principle of the preservation and development of
the Canadian social and economic union.

(2) The preservation and development of the social union
includes, but is not limited to, the following policy objectives:

(a) providing throughout Canada a health care system
that is comprehensive, universal, portable, publicly
administered, and accessible.

---

* As released October 9, 1992. A best efforts text prepared by officials
representing all the First Ministers and Aboriginal and Territorial Leaders.

(b) providing adequate social services and benefits to ensure that all individuals resident in Canada have reasonable access to housing, food and other basic necessities;

(c) providing high quality primary and secondary education to all individuals resident in Canada and ensuring reasonable access to post-secondary education;

(d) protecting the rights of workers to organize and bargain collectively; and

(e) protecting, preserving and sustaining the integrity of the environment for present and future generations.

(3) The preservation and development of the economic union includes, but is not limited to, the following policy objectives:

(a) working together to strengthen the Canadian economic union;

(b) the free movement of persons, goods, services and capital;

(c) the goal of full employment;

(d) ensuring that all Canadians have a reasonable standard of living; and

(e) ensuring sustainable and equitable development.

(4) This Part does not have the effect of modifying the interpretation of the rights and freedoms referred to in the *Canadian Charter of Rights and Freedoms*.

36.2 The Prime Minister of Canada and the first ministers of the provinces shall, at a conference convened pursuant to section 37.1, establish a mechanism to monitor the progress made in relation to the objectives stated in subsections 36.1(2) and (3).

MARQUIS
Montmagny, Qc
November 1992